Art Nouveau silver buckle, c. 1900.

A turn-of-the-century horn and gold hair comb by Georges Fouquet; the comb is set with opals and enamel.

TONY CURTIS
WITH ELISABETH D TAYLOR

CHARTWELL
BOOKS, INC.

A QUARTO BOOK

Published by Chartwell Books
A Division of Book Sales, Inc.
110 Enterprise Avenue
Secaucus, New Jersey 07094

ISBN 1-55521-523-8

This book was designed and produced by
Quarto Publishing plc
The Old Brewery, 6 Blundell Street
London N7 9BH

Senior Editor Susanna Clarke
Editors Charyn Jones, Mary Chesshyre
Technical Consultant Vivienne Couldrey
Designer John Grain
Picture Researchers Anne Marie Ehrlich, Deirdre O'Day

Art Director Moira Clinch
Editorial Director Carolyn King

Typeset by Aptimage Ltd
Manufactured in Hong Kong by Regent Publishing
Services Ltd
Printed by Leefung-Asco Printers Ltd, Hong Kong

Contents

Foreword

ONCE UPON A TIME, as the old story goes, antique collectors turned up their noses at anything that was not a least 100 years old. Today that attitude is as outdated as a fairy tale; some of the most desirable objects in the collecting world were bought by our parents and grandparents — and even by ourselves.

Part of the fascination of the 20th century as a period for collectors is the possibility that, lying in a cabinet or hidden upstairs in the attic, there could be an unsuspected treasure. Not only that, but in the local store there could be something that will be a pleasure to own and become a collecting treasure in the future.

When housewives in the 1930s were picking cheap crockery painted by Clarice Cliff or Susie Cooper off the counters of dime stores, they would have been astonished to be told that their children would have to pay hundreds of dollars for one plate. When fond parents of the 1960s gave their children Japanese wind-up toys for Christmas, how could they guess that, only twenty years later, a buyer of the same toy would pay well over $1000 for it?

The man or woman who saved menu cards from Miss Cranston's Glasgow tearooms may or may not have known that they were designed by Margaret Macdonald, wife of Charles Rennie Mackintosh, but they did not imagine that one card would change hands for $800 in the 1980s. It is a good thing that the hard-up Mackintosh himself had no ink-ling that the electroplated teaspoons he designed for the same tearooms would sell for $420 a spoon and that one of his white lacquered chairs would be fought over by collectors willing to pay more than $35,000 to secure it.

It was the desire to keep a souvenir of his heroes that made a Beatles fan in the 1960s save a cheap tin of Beatles talc by Margo of Mayfair, but twenty years later the tin was to be worth $85.

Another element of 20th century collecting that is important is that it provides a glimpse of social history. The things that people bought and treasured can be seen as a reflection of social trends and developments.

During the 19th century, the rise in the standard of living for the majority of people was mirrored by a growing awareness on the part of manufacturers of the spending power of ordinary people. This mushroomed in the 20th century and the luxury market became less important than it had been when money was concentrated in the hands of a minority.

Jewelry is an excellent indicator of this change. At the beginning of the century jewelers catered almost exclusively to the rich, but as the trend began to change, imitation jewelry made of paste, glass, cultured pearls, and other cheaper materials took over. There was still a luxury market of course, catering to people like Edward VIII and Mrs Simpson, but the pieces they commissioned were copied in cheaper

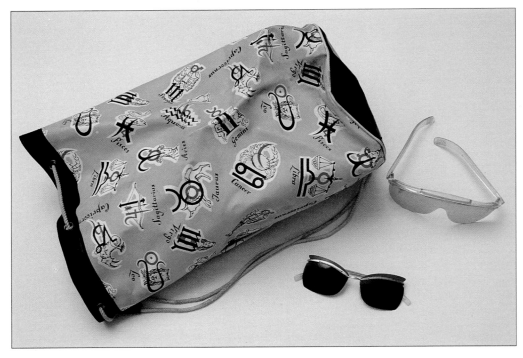

From the era of angry young men and duffel coats, a 1950s plastic duffel bag. Sunglasses became a symbol of design consciousness in the 1960s, a time of popular package vacations in the sun.

| COST | ● ● |
| OUTLOOK | ● ● ● |

New inventions inspired stunningly original design concepts like this Ekco Model A22 radio, designed by Wells Coats in 1945. It still has a modern look and is highly prized today.

COST	● ● ●
OUTLOOK	● ● ● ●

materials so shop girls could sport bracelets and earrings in the same styles. Today jewelers are continuing this trend by working in acrylic, nylon, rubber, and stainless steel. A brooch does not have to be made of gold and set with diamonds to be worth wearing — and collecting.

The unemployment and Depression that followed World War I were countered by a massive amount of housebuilding. The new homes were not for the rich but for the middle and lower middle classes who, once they became home owners, wanted to keep up with fashion and filled their rooms with furniture and ornaments. The things they bought — flying ducks, Lloyd Loom furniture, floor rugs in abstract designs, wooden-cased radios and Doulton ornamental figures — are among today's prestige collectibles.

The amazing upsurge of interest in collecting artifacts of the 20th century does not, however, mean that nothing should ever be thrown away: the secret of collecting for the future is to develop a discriminating eye. Once you are attuned to appreciating objects of beauty and ingenuity, prizes can be spotted in very unlikely places.

Some people collect labels off food cans but they are particular about what they save, concentrating on labels that show a high degree of artistry or mark a change in popular eating habits. There are others who collect posters, but again they look for what is fresh, original, or highly artistic. The posters done by Cassandre for 1930s ocean liners are elegant, simple, and evocative of that streamlined age; the jokey posters Fougasse produced for Guinness bring back the atmosphere of life in the 1950s and 60s.

HOW TO USE THIS BOOK

Collectors should remember that, in the 1920s, someone had the discrimination to buy a Chiparus figure or a Leach pot for a fraction of its present-day price. Today they can enjoy searching out attractive or intriguing objects that appear on the market now for a few dollars but that may be worth a lot more in the future.

The collectibles in this book have been given a "star" rating (indicated by disks) that will help you familiarize yourself with the sort of prices you can expect to pay and the experts' opinion of their value as an investment.

COST GUIDE
The cost rating is given first and each object has been put into one of five categories.

COST	
●	$1-20
● ●	$21-200
● ● ●	$201-2000
● ● ● ●	$2001-10,000
● ● ● ● ●	$10,000 plus

OUTLOOK GUIDE
While no one can predict with certainty how much the worth of a particular piece is likely to increase, our outlook rating gives you expert guidance on estimated rise in value over the next ten to fifteen years. Once again each piece has been graded with one to five "stars": one "star" for modest gains, up to five "stars" for what promises to be a very worthwhile investment indeed. The star grading is based on the current value of the piece: thus a relatively inexpensive china teapot that seems set to double or treble its value over the next decade has been given a greater outlook rating than a piece of expensive jewelry that will rise in value by a small percentage of its current worth.

Today it is still possible to pick out what is going to be a treasure of the future and, by owning it, enhance your life at the same time. That is what 20th century collecting is all about.

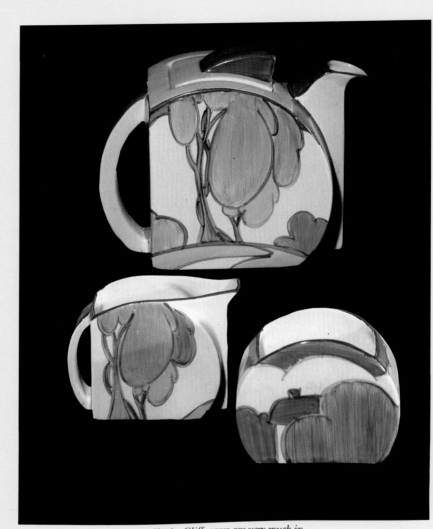

Clarice Cliff wares are very much in favor, particularly pre-1935 designs like this Fantasque tea-for-two service, 1931.

CHAPTER ONE

China & Ceramics

ORNAMENTAL FIGURES

DOULTON CHARACTER JUGS

SMALL POTTERIES

CHINA PAINTERS

CELEBRATION & ADVERTISING

GOSS & ITS COMPETITORS

TEAPOTS

MODERN POTTERS

Introduction

THERE CAN HARDLY be a household that does not contain a piece of china that is worth far more than the owner realizes. After 1900, with increased spending power among the working classes, there was a great upsurge in the popular buying of chinaware. Manufacturers found that modern factory methods helped them cater for this new demand, and designers began to exercise their imaginations to produce new lines to capture the fancy of buyers without large sums of money to spend. The huge expansion of stores like Woolworths was also partly responsible for putting pretty china in every home, and it is interesting that some of today's most eagerly sought-after pieces — particularly the works of Susie Cooper and Clarice Cliff — were originally sold for pennies in such dime stores.

The last ten years have seen a tremendous rise in the prices of pieces that hardly raised any interest in the early 1970s but what was then dismissed as "1930s junk" is now vying with Wedgwood and Meissen for the attention of specialists.

China is a popular field for collecting because there is vast choice and attractive things can be found in all price ranges. Some very specialized items do cost thousands but modest enthusiasts, having selected a specialty, can build up an interesting collection without breaking the bank.

Taste is always changing, and there is always something new to find. It is possible to specialize in unusual glazes, or in the work of original painters, or the output of special factories. On the other hand, some people search out the work of talented studio potters for, after all, even Bernard Leach was once an unknown, struggling for recognition. The secret is to spot well-designed, attractive, and unusual pieces and to have the courage to put your money where your eye tells you.

An Indian portrait vase from Rockwood Standard glaze pottery, decorated by Grace Young, 1905.

Goss vacation souvenir china in the shape of Wordsworth's Dove Cottage at Grasmere.

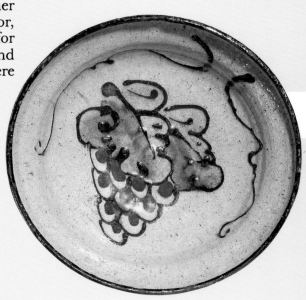

A rare and important soft raku bowl by leading potter Bernard Leach.

A Clarice Cliff oval serving dish painted with the Chaldane design by John Armstrong for Harrods, 1934.

Earthenware figure by M. Pavolwy made in 1907 for Wiener Keramik.

Bara ware vase by William Moorcroft for Liberty's, 1907.

New German designs broke free from tradition in the 1930s.

The first Royal Doulton character jug John Barleycorn 1934 (left) with Samuel Johnson and Izaak Walton.

Stoneware coffee service by Lucie Rie c. 1956.

Prince Charles Mug, 1981, from Carlton Ware.

Glazed stoneware by Richard De Vore, taking a bold new line.

A large-footed bowl in earthenware with classical inspiration by Beatrice Wood, 1987.

Ornamental Figures

ABOVE *Pottery figures capture the grace and elegance of their era: a Goldscheider pottery figure of a dancer, 1930, made in Austria.*

COST	● ●
OUTLOOK	● ●

WHILE THE EMPHASIS of avant-garde china and pottery was on vases, bowls, and tableware, there was always a strong popular market for figures of birds, animals, and people. Only a few artists managed to bridge the gap between the old style and the new, notably Dutchman Josef Mendes da Costa, who made elegant, stately figures in rough clay with pitted surfaces painted in pale colors.

Because of the artistic reaction against Victorian taste, Meissen figures, which had enjoyed a huge following in the previous two centuries, were out of fashion except among specialists, but recently they have been back in favor. Like Sèvres, who produced figures by Rodin, Leonard, and Jean Gauguin, the Meissen company has continued to make its figures of children and mythological groups.

Also in Europe, the Danish Royal Porcelain Manufactory of Copenhagen brought out statuettes by Kund Kyhn, while at the Bavarian factory, established in the late 19th century by Philip Rosenthal, remarkable Art Deco figures of pierrots were being made during the 1920s and 1930s.

The "wedding present" market encouraged Royal Worcester to produce a wide range of figures by artists like Dorothy Doughty, Doris Lindner, Aline Ellis, Eric Aumonier, and Frederick Gertner, who sculpted pretty children and military figures. They also introduced modern fashion into their lines with copies of Japanese netsuke, figures of animals in "Old Ivory" glaze, which proved so popular that some — particularly the rabbit and the mouse — continued in production until the 1950s.

Royal Doulton's ornamental figures, long regarded as the preferred purchases of middle-class housewives, have come into collecting prominence since the early 1980s. The company has produced over 2000 different models and the collecting fever for them is now high in America, Canada, and Australia. Figures made in short ranges are most desirable, so "Polly Peachum" and "Rose," which were produced in thousands, are worth less than Charles Noke's short-run model "Katherine." Royal Wedgwood and Derby also produced figures and models that are being collected now. Make sure there are no hairline cracks in any models you buy because these cut the price by more than 50 percent.

After World War I, the Ashtead Pottery in Sussex was established to provide work for disabled servicemen and produced white, glazed earthenware figures standing on garlands of blue, yellow, and maroon flowers. These figures were cheap enough to bring them within the reach of the mass market. Also popular were the Czechoslovakian figures, particularly of football players, which sold in the 1920s and 1930s for about a quarter and are now worth much more.

ABOVE *Doulton figures also reflect popular culture: porcelain figure of Bat Girl, c. 1927, by Dan Klein.*

COST	● ●
OUTLOOK	● ●

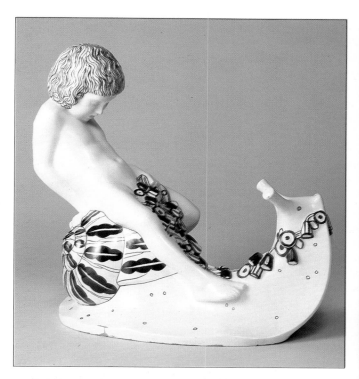

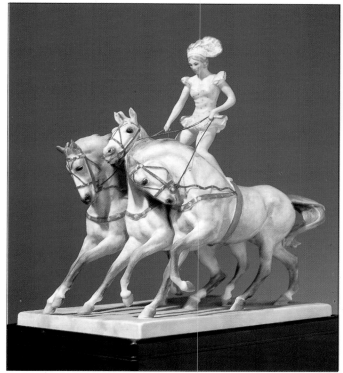

TOP LEFT *Earthenware figure modeled by M. Pavolwy for Wiener Keramik, c. 1907.*

COST	● ● ●
OUTLOOK	● ● ● ●

ABOVE *HRH The Duchess of York in her wedding gown; this is a fine bone china model in a limited edition sculpted by Eric Griffiths for Royal Doulton.*

COST	● ●
OUTLOOK	● ●

BELOW LEFT *"In the Ring," — modeled by Doris Lindner — a rare model introduced by Royal Worcester Spode in 1937.*

COST	● ● ●
OUTLOOK	● ●

Doulton Character Jugs

ROYAL DOULTON launched their range of character jugs in 1934 with John Barleycorn, designed by Charles Noke, which went on being produced in large numbers and various sizes until 1960.

There is a huge range of Doulton jugs, including some modeled on movie stars like Mae West, Clark Gable, and Charlie Chaplin, on figures from Dickens like Sairey Gamp, or on historical figures like Sir Winston Churchill and Sir Francis Drake. Some of the early models are still in production but most were discontinued in the 1960s — and that, of course, makes them all the more collectible today.

Doulton character jugs have now become a very specialized market and variations in design determine a jug's rarity and consequently its value. Small details such as the colors of buttons, triangles, or hair can mean the difference between hundreds and thousands of dollars for an individual jug. For example if Harry Fenton's Sir Francis Drake is not wearing a hat, the jug will be worth more than twenty times as much as his Drake with a hat.

Some of the most valuable jugs are plain white because they were "seconds," sold only to employees, and many were never developed commercially so are very rare. Another rarity is the cream-colored "loving cup" jug with black handles modeled by Noke on the head of Winston Churchill, never produced in large numbers and finally withdrawn because the famous statesman was not pleased with his likeness.

BELOW *The first Royal Doulton character jug John Barleycorn (left), designed by Charles Noke, was made from 1934 to 1960. Others were: Samuel Johnson (center), designed by Harry Fenton (1950) and made for 10 years; Izaak Walton, designed by Geoff Blower, in production 1953-82.*

COST	● ● ●
OUTLOOK	● ● ●

TOP RIGHT *Three Toby character jugs. Good modeling, coloring, and unusual features all increase value.*

COST	● ●
OUTLOOK	● ● ●

BELOW RIGHT *The Ronald Reagan character jug was produced by Royal Doulton in 1984 in a limited edition, the first time a United States President had joined the character jug collection.*

COST	● ● ●
OUTLOOK	● ● ● ●

Celebrity Jugs

W. C. Fields and Mae West are part of "The Celebrity Collection," a series of six character jugs made by Royal Doulton which were first issued as a promotional item for American Express in 1983. Groucho Marx, Jimmy Durante, and Louis Armstrong were also featured, but the Clark Gable jug, designed by Stan Taylor and numbered D6709, was withdrawn in 1984 because of copyright difficulties — though not before around fifty had already been sold. As a result this rare item is now worth upward of $4000 while the others in the series sell for around $85.

Small Potteries

ADMIRATION FOR JAPANESE ART first established itself in Europe after the Paris Exhibition of 1862. In the 1920s Japan was the main source of inspiration for Bernard Leach who was a leading figure in the European and American modern movement in pottery making. His work had a much newer look than anything that had gone before, with its simple shapes and misty, blue-green glazes, and it influenced a selection of talented young potters, including his son David and his wife Janet Darnell, who made pots shaped like melons or gourds with small apertures in the top in rugged natural textures, often with glaze spilling down the sides like fondant icing.

The Leach style is still influential, and among his most highly regarded disciples was Geoffrey Whiting who died in 1988. But Leach also had followers in unexpected places; a few years ago, when forgeries of his pots were turning up for sale, they were traced to a prison workshop where prisoners had been carrying occupational therapy to unexpected lengths.

As well as inspiring the prison inmates, Leach influenced Lucie Rie, Hans Coper, Paul Metcalfe, Michael Cardew, Katherine Pleydell-Bouverie, Norah Braden, Elizabeth Fritsch, Ewan Henderson, Dorothy Feibler, Gordon Baldwin, Alison Britton, Martin Smith, Carol McNicholl, Janice Tchalenko, Magdalene Odundo, Alan Caier-Smith, Linda Gunn-Russell, Fiona Salazar, Wally Keeler, and, in America, Voulkos, Betty Woodman, Jerry Rothman, and Viola Frey.

In America the enthusiasm for pottery making had a rich flowering. Of six thriving potteries in Cincinnati, Ohio, in the 1880s, the most famous was the Rookwood Pottery, founded by Mrs. Maria Longworth Nichols. When the pottery won a Grand Prix at the 1900 Paris Exhibition, a craze started for its elegant vases, tiles, medallions, and plaques decorated with floral themes or pictures of Indians, Negroes, animals, and birds. The Rookwood Pottery went bankrupt in 1941, however, and Artus van Briggle, an artist from Rookwood, started his own pottery in Colorado Springs making Art Nouveau pieces with a glowing matte finish. He died in 1904 and the work was carried on by his artist wife.

At Zanesville, Ohio, the Lonhuda Pottery, for which designer Laura Fry and Jacques Sicard worked, produced the Aurelian and Eocean ranges, decorated with flowers, fruit, animals, and Indians, as well as Sicardo with its rich metallic lusters in purples, greens, and browns.

In New Orleans, the Newcomb Pottery opened in 1897 as an adjunct to the Sophie Newcomb Memorial College for Women with Miss Mary Sheerer, director of the college, as its designer. Its specialty was clean, elegant shapes, glazed in misty colors and with decorations inspired by local flowers, especially the magnolia.

Other notable American potteries include the Chelsea Keramic Works of Chelsea, Massachusetts, which copied oriental glazes on its Dedham Ware; the Roseville Pottery Co. of Zanesville, which made a wide range of art pottery; the Pewabic Pottery of M. C. Perry in Detroit, Michigan; and the Grueby Faience and Tile Co. of Boston which made heavy pottery decorated with plants in low relief and a monochrome finish.

TOP LEFT *Porcelain pots by Lucie Rie, c. 1955.*

| COST | ● ● ● |
| OUTLOOK | ● ● ● ● |

TOP RIGHT *Rookwood vase.*

| COST | ● ● ● ● |
| OUTLOOK | ● ● ● ● |

RIGHT *White glazed porcelain bottle vase by Lucie Rie, c. 1974.*

| COST | ● ● ● |
| OUTLOOK | ● ● ● |

FAR RIGHT *Collection of stoneware vases and a cup by Hans Coper.*

| COST | ● ● ● |
| OUTLOOK | ● ● ● |

OPPOSITE LEFT *Stoneware pilgrim dish and leaping salmon vase by Bernard Leach.*

| COST | ● ● ● |
| OUTLOOK | ● ● ● |

OPPOSITE RIGHT *Stoneware bottles by Bernard Leach.*

| COST | ● ● ● |
| OUTLOOK | ● ● ● |

China Painters

THE SUCCESS ENJOYED by the Barlow sisters at Doulton in the 19th century paved the way for a new generation of talented women china painters.

Susie Cooper started out as a fashion designer before turning her hand to pottery in the 1920s. Her style was only deceptively naïve, deriving from the work of painters like Vuillard and Picasso, and she married this to everyday subjects such as thatched cottages and pretty gardens. She made incised stoneware jugs, bowls, and vases for A. E. Gray, and the few that have survived are very expensive because a fire in her stockroom destroyed much of her output. However, when she started her own company in 1932, she produced a wide range of tableware in startling, highly colored, geometric designs that commanded a mass market and was sold in dime stores.

Clarice Cliff worked for the Wilkinson Pottery from 1930 to 1938 when she joined the Burslem-based Newport Pottery for whom she continued to work till the 1950s. Her designs were fresh and original, reflecting the mood of her times, and she was particularly influenced by Serge Diaghilev's Ballets Russes. She gave her lines titles like Bizarre, Ravel, Delicia, Café Au Lait, and Gayday, and they were highly evocative of the feeling of the Jazz Age. Some of her rarer, one-of-a-kind pieces, like her self-portrait vase and a Ballet Russes plate, are now worth a great deal of money.

Charlotte Rhead (1885-1947), who came from a famous ceramics family, worked for three potters, Wood and Sons of Bursley, Burgess and Leigh, and, finally, A. G. Richardson, producing a wide range of tube-lined work, particularly chargers, jugs, and vases. Her pieces were painted with either geometric or floral themes. Daisy Makeig-Jones, who was probably the most fey of all the female artists, produced intricately painted, dreamlike "Fairyland Lustre" plaques for Wedgwood.

In Scotland, artists like Jessie Marion King, Elizabeth Mary Watt, Ann McBeth, and Helen Watson tried their hand at pottery making, and some of their pieces can still be picked up for very reasonable prices. The most sought after is Jessie Marion King, whose work is identified by her mark of a rabbit and a gate.

LEFT *A Clarice Cliff plate — one of a set of three with a design by Laura Knight of a circus girl on horseback, 1934.*

COST	● ● ● ●
OUTLOOK	● ● ● ●

RIGHT *A Susie Cooper figurine and ginger jar, c. 1925.*

COST	● ● ●
OUTLOOK	● ● ● ●

BELOW *A vase by Charlotte Rhead for Crown Ducal Potteries, c. 1930.*

COST	● ● ●
OUTLOOK	● ● ●

Clarice Cliff

Born in 1899 in Staffordshire, Clarice Cliff started work at the age of thirteen painting freehand on to pottery at one of the local factories. In 1928, after studying sculpture at the Royal College of Art, she went to work for the Newport Pottery where she persuaded her boss Colley Shorter to allow her to hand-paint sixty dozen pieces to test the market at a trade fair. So popular did her designs prove to be that within a year the whole factory was employed making her Bizarre Ware. One of her finest pieces is a wall plaque decorated with a scene inspired by Diaghilev's costume design for the Ballets Russes, which sold at Christie's for £8000.

Celebration & Advertising

ABOVE *Silent Night — first of a series of six Christmas Plates by Royal Doulton.*

COST	●
OUTLOOK	●

RIGHT *Royal Doulton Historical Promotions produced this bone china beaker, 3¾in (95mm) high, inscribed "Coronation King Edward VII June 1902." The beaker has rarity value because the coronation had to be postponed to August due to the illness of the King with appendicitis.*

COST	● ● ●
OUTLOOK	● ● ●

ABOVE *Prince Charles mug — a humorous Royal Wedding souvenir by Marc for Carlton Ware.*

COST	● ●
OUTLOOK	● ● ●

TOP RIGHT *Small and amusing animals produced to commemorate the investiture of Charles as Prince of Wales in 1969. Series by John Beswick.*

COST	●
OUTLOOK	●

BELOW RIGHT *Wedgwood have a long tradition of commemorative china. This set in characteristic blue jasper marked the wedding of Prince Andrew and Sarah Ferguson in 1987.*

COST	● ●
OUTLOOK	● ●

THE VOGUE FOR COLLECTING china commemorating some special royal occasion reached its peak during the reign of Queen Victoria. In the early 19th century the Royal Family was viewed with, at best, indifference, but Queen Victoria's long reign and her grim determination "to be good" made her into something of a household goddess, and it was considered patriotic to display a plate or a mug painted with her unsmiling visage on the mantelpiece.

China manufacturers both in Britain and abroad cashed in on the new demand. Potteries like Wedgwood, Coalport, Aynsley, and Minton turned out commemoratives, while cheaper ones were imported from Austria. Coronations and royal marriages were the primary occasions for the making of mugs, plates, and loving cups painted with the Royal Arms or a likeness of the person being honored. The coronation that never happened — that of Edward VIII, which would have taken place in 1937 but never did because of his abdication —

Brewers and Distillers

Give-away china was an excellent way of getting free advertising which was particularly used by brewers and distillers. Collectors today pay good prices for any of these that have survived. Among their favorites are the striding figure of Johnny Walker — "still going strong" — and the ornament used to advertise White Horse whisky which was seen in pubs and hotels up and down England. Decorated whisky flagons made of china, often by Doultons, were also widely distributed. Cream of the Barley whisky, for example, was sold in a brown glazed jar with an embossed decoration. Doultons also made ceramic plaques and painted china beer handles advertising special beers or bearing the name of a particular inn. Guinness was a great user of advertising give-aways and the tableware painted with a toucan, which they gave out promoting their ale, is among the most coveted advertising china to be found today. Also look out for their ashtrays and china jugs. From a collecting point of view, Guinness is very good for you.

is recorded in many cups, plates, and mugs that were produced in advance by hopeful china factories. Unfortunately they are not rare and therefore not particularly valuable.

The extensiveness of the present Royal Family makes it a good source of inspiration for commemorative objects, and the big occasions of their lives are guaranteed to keep china store registers ringing. The wedding of Elizabeth and Philip, their Silver Wedding, Charles's Investiture, Anne's wedding, the marriages of Charles and Diana and Andrew and Sarah have all brought forth a flood of china mementoes, ranging from the expensive and elegant to the cheap and cheerful.

In America, there was also a demand for commemorative china honoring various Presidents. Some of them were made in the U.S. by Patriotic Products of Syracuse, but many others were exported in large quantities from British potteries in Burslem, Staffordshire.

Goss & its Competitors

THE MOST FAMOUS producers of "cheap and cheerful" pottery, which flooded the market in the first half of the 20th century, was the Stoke-on-Trent-based pottery of W. H. Goss. They produced miniature pieces of crested china to sell to vacationers at a nickel or a dime a time. William Henry Goss and his enterprising son, Adolphus, the "Goss Boss," recognized an enormous market in the new mobility brought about by the expansion of the railroad network. For the first time people were taking vacations away from home and wanted souvenirs to remind them of their two weeks by the sea. So, in the 1880s, Goss started his most popular lines of small, cheap models of everything from trains to lighthouses marked with the crests of each town or district. The company enjoyed tremendous success until 1929 when Goss sold out to Cauldron Potteries. They produced more than 2500 different shapes, and Adolphus appointed an agent in each town and district to sell pieces painted with local crests. A collecting craze began with people seeking out examples of each crest or shape, and Adolphus made sure that if they wanted a piece with the crest of Inverness, they had to go to the town to buy it.

The most pricey of the Goss products were the fifty-one miniature cottages — particularly models of famous ones like the Priest's House, Prestbury, or Sulgrave Manor, Northamptonshire — which were expensive at around sixty cents but proved to be a good investment: today they bring prices that run into four figures.

Goss's good idea had many imitators including Carlton Ware, best known for its 1920s porcelain with bright enameling and gilding on black backgrounds, marked with a swallow inside a circle and topped with a crown. Other Goss competitors were Arcadian, Ford's China, Grafton China, Macintyre, Podmore, Savoy, Nautilus, and Shelley of which Foley's was a subsidiary company. Shelley Ltd. made figures of sportsmen, models of ancient buildings and monuments, vehicles, characters from history and fiction, and models of animals and birds.

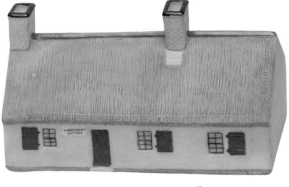

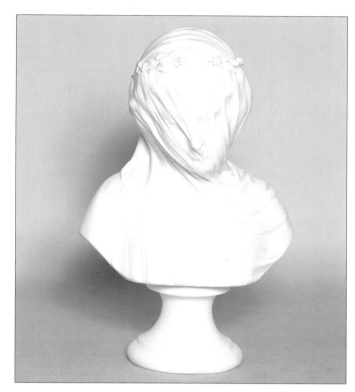

LEFT *Goss China bust — "The Veiled Bride."*

COST	● ● ●
OUTLOOK	● ●

BELOW *Crested wares — produced as souvenirs for the early tourist market.*

COST	●
OUTLOOK	● ●

Almost every piece of Goss china is named and has a factory mark, making collecting easier.

TOP LEFT *Christchurch Old Court House.*

COST	● ● ●
OUTLOOK	● ●

TOP RIGHT *Robert Burns' House..*

COST	● ●
OUTLOOK	● ●

BOTTOM LEFT *St. Catherine's Chapel, Abbotsbury, Devon.*

COST	● ● ●
OUTLOOK	● ●

BOTTOM RIGHT *Priest's House, Prestbury, England.*

COST	● ● ●
OUTLOOK	● ●

Teapots

SAMUEL PEPYS NOTED in his Diary the day he drank his first cup of tea, but for many years tea was only available to the upper classes — at least until the duty on imported tea was slashed in the mid-18th century and it became a favorite drink. Infuriated that they were denied cheap tea, Americans even went to war because they had to pay too much duty on it.

In the 20th century "a nice cup of tea" has continued to be a symbol of comfort and prosperity, served from a huge variety of teapots that range from elegant copies of 18th-century Meissen pots to those made in the shape of racing cars.

Every pottery specializing in tableware made teapots and today examples of Susie Cooper's or Clarice Cliff's artistry are greatly prized; the teapot Dr. Christopher Dresser designed for Linthorpe Pottery is among highly desired collectibles and, after the modern movement began, potters like Lucie

Rie turned out elegant stoneware teapots in Japanese shapes, often with wickerwork handles.

In the 1930s a great vogue began for "jokey" teapots, and although some of them did not pour very well, they were accorded pride of place in the china cabinets of many middle-class families. They came in every shape and size — elephants with their trunks as spouts, thatched cottages, flowers, posturing clowns, fire engines, and steam trains.

Teapots were also made by souvenir manufacturers and stamped with the names of vacation resorts or embossed with figures of Cornish pixies, kilted Highlanders, or Welsh women in tall black hats.

Teapots make a marvelous field for collectors because there are so many of them about, and amusing or pretty examples can be found in all price ranges.

ABOVE *British car teapot, 1930s.*

COST	● ●	
OUTLOOK	● ●	

OPPOSITE: TOP LEFT *British elephant teapot, 1980s.*

COST	● ●	
OUTLOOK	● ●	

TOP RIGHT *Clarice Cliff teapot designed by Eva Crofts, 1934.*

COST	● ● ●	
OUTLOOK	● ● ●	

CENTER *Whiteware shell teapot by Anne Kraus, 1986.*

COST	● ● ●	
OUTLOOK	● ● ●	

Modern Potters

THERE IS SO MUCH collectible pottery that it has become essential for collectors to specialize in a defined area. It could be the work of a particular potter or studio, a particular time or geographical area, a special type of object, or a favorite color. Country potteries in Britain, for example, were established early this century in places as far apart as Rye in Sussex and Kirkaldy in Fife, and each has its individual characteristics, such as decorations of rustic hops or emblem thistles.

Bernard Leach was the father figure and most celebrated practitioner of the modern studio-pottery movement. In his St. Ives pottery he set standards of quality, blending classical oriental and traditional English pottery. Thanks to him, studio-potteries flourished in England, and his pupils and followers have included many famous potters, such as Michael Cardew and Michael Casson.

After World War II there were important new influences from Europe, led by Lucie Rie, Hans Coper, and Elizabeth Fritsch. Pottery increasingly became a medium of free artistic expression.

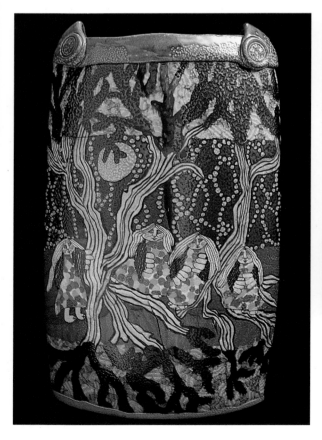

LEFT *Hand-built vase by Jane Feiser.*

COST	●	●	●
OUTLOOK	●	●	

ABOVE *Glaze-decorated stoneware bowl, 14in (36cm) in diameter, by Janice Tchalenko.*

COST	●	●	●
OUTLOOK	●	●	●

Blue stoneware form by Alan Peascod, Australia.

COST	● ● ●
OUTLOOK	● ● ● ●

Moorcroft Pottery

When some bright spark at James Macintyre & Co. decided in 1913 to switch production from pottery to the new-fangled electrical goods, their pottery designer, William Moorcroft, was left a little short of work, to say the least. So with fifteen years of experience behind him, and bearing in mind that life begins at forty, Moorcroft took the plunge and established his own pottery works at Cobridge, near Stoke-on-Trent, employing many of his former colleagues from Macintyre's. Without any restraints, he could give free rein to his ideas, leaving a legacy of distinctive pottery much sought after today. All his products bear his signature, W. Moorcroft — usually in green until 1920 and thereafter mainly in blue — together with the impressed mark Moorcroft or Moorcroft Burslem.

LEFT *Hand-built, burnished and polished red clay vase by Magdalene Anyango Namakhiya Odundo, 1985.*

COST	● ●
OUTLOOK	● ●

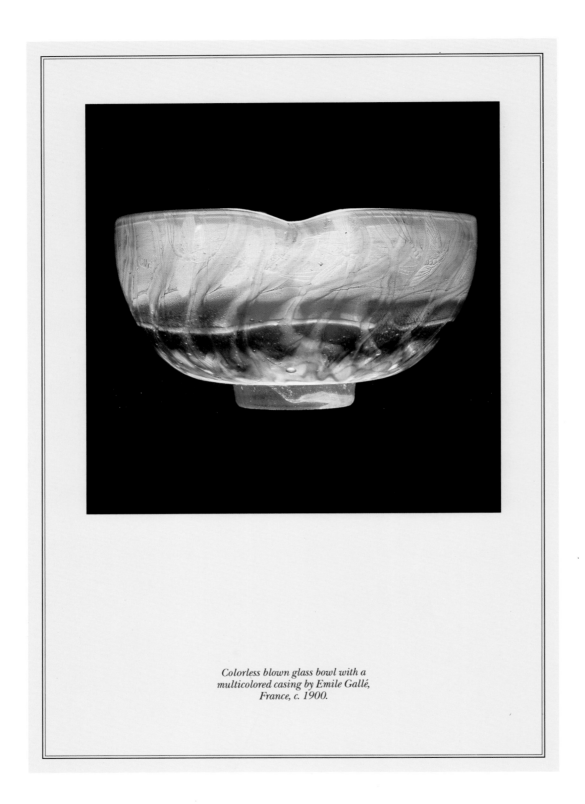

*Colorless blown glass bowl with a
multicolored casing by Emile Gallé,
France, c. 1900.*

CHAPTER TWO

Glass

LALIQUE & FOLLOWERS

TIFFANY, GALLÉ, & FOLLOWERS

AMERICAN GLASS

SCANDINAVIAN GLASS

GLASSES & BOTTLES

STAINED GLASS

Introduction

Flower form vase with slender stem and iridescent color in blown glass by L.C. Tiffany & Co., 1905.

AT THE BEGINNING OF THE 20TH CENTURY glassmaking was undergoing a revolution that was to transform people's perception of glass. The artistic imagination and technical virtuosity of the new generation of glassmakers brought a sunburst of color and vivacity into what had become a stagnant art form.

This revolution was not entirely novel, for much of its inspiration came from the ancient past, from Roman and early Middle Eastern glassmakers. The new glassmakers rejected the ponderous, deeply cut glass of the 19th century and turned instead to new shapes, some of them modeled on swanlike Persian rose-water sprinklers, or tried to reproduce surfaces that looked as if they had spent a thousand years buried beneath the ground. They molded, sculpted, and pressed glass like the plastic medium it is — not the stiff material that it had been rendered by Victorian glassmakers.

These new artists had a huge background of knowledge and styles to call upon because glassmaking is an ancient art. The technique of fusing a silica with an alkali before blowing, and then molding or pressing it into the desired shape was practiced in Asia four centuries before Christ. The achievement of the new glassmakers was to turn those ancient forms and methods into something new and exciting. This excitement and sense of experimentation strikes us today when we look at the glassware of artists like Gallé, Tiffany, Lalique, and Henri Cros. Their achievement was that the pieces they created when the century began are still avant-garde today. Because they have also never been rivaled, it is fair to describe the early years of the 20th century as the golden age of glass.

L'Oiseau de Feu — molded glass lamp by René Lalique, France 1925.

Paperweight in green and white filigree glass, Italy, c. 1950.

"The Overflowing Landscape," blown glass blank, stipple engraved, by Laurence Whistler, England, 1974.

Art Nouveau pâte-de-verre shaped cylindrical vase by Gabriel Argy-Rousseau.

Glass vase by Daum of Nancy, France. The frame of wrought iron was by Louis Majorelle, c. 1920.

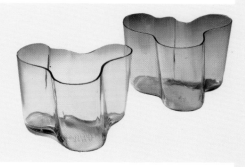

Ceylan Vase, c. 1925, a translucent bluish-yellow opal glass by René Lalique & Cie, France.

Opaque black glass vase with Rockwell silver decoration, United States, c. 1925-38.

Savoy and Karhula glass vases designed by Alvar Aalto, c. 1940.

Iittala glass dish, cast and polished by Tapio Wirkkala, Finland, c. 1952.

Glass handkerchief vase by Vernini; a striking new shape in the 1950s.

Free-form glass vase with amber center.

Morning Glory on a trellis paperweight by Charles Kazium, United States, c. 1980.

Three-piece Alexandrite sculpture, designed by Ludvika Smrckova, Czechoslovakia, 1982.

Lalique & Followers

THE GENIUS OF René Lalique was that his work has never gone out of date. He started a movement that influences our lives today because his artistry was applied across a vast spectrum and he saw nothing wrong in allying art and industry.

He started his career as a jeweler but, in 1908, when he was invited to design perfume bottles for Coty, he quickly realized the possibilities of mass production and opened a glass factory near Paris. The Coty association led to his making bottles of unprecedented style and beauty for a wide range of other perfume manufacturers, and customers would often buy certain brands more for the bottle than the scent inside it.

Lalique's work has two main distinguishing marks; firstly, he wanted to create new and interesting surfaces and used sand or acid blasting techniques to make his glass look opalescent. Secondly, his imagination allowed him to create original designs and bring a new dimension to glassmaking. By molding the glass, he could relate his motifs to the shape of the piece; plants, animals, or female figures curved with ease and elegance around his work. Bowls were decorated with swirling fish and vases were embellished with parakeets, as can be seen in his "Ceylan" vase. The *line* was all-important.

Because he was an astute businessman, Lalique was always eager to grasp opportunities to use glass in unusual ways. Not only did he make light fixtures, clocks, decorative pieces, tableware, and jewelry, but he also designed glass car mascots. It probably never occurred to him that these would become some of the most desirable collectibles in the glass world. Mascots were made in a wide variety of shapes, including hawks and cockerels, but the most famous is his "Victoire," or "The Spirit of the Wind," exalting the female form.

His factory is still in existence at Wingen-sur-Moder, but the "R" from his signature was omitted after his death in 1945. René Lalique was one of the founders of what is known as the Art Nouveau movement and had, and still has, many imitators, the best of whom include Sabino, Ething and Verlys.

ABOVE *Tête d'Eprevier — Lalique car mascot in opalescent glass.*

COST	● ● ● ●
OUTLOOK	● ● ● ●

OPPOSITE PAGE *Victoire — the record-breaking Lalique car mascot, amethyst-tinted.*

COST	● ● ● ● ●
OUTLOOK	● ● ● ●

TOP LEFT *A blue glass table clock — "Le Jour et Le Nuit" — by René Lalique 14³⁄₄in (37cm) high.*

COST	● ● ● ●
OUTLOOK	● ● ● ●

TOP RIGHT *"Coq nain" — Lalique car mascot in purple glass.*

COST	● ● ● ●
OUTLOOK	● ● ● ●

BOTTOM LEFT *Peacock lamp of clear glass, acid etched and ribbed and decorated with peacocks. Signed by René Lalique, 1925.*

COST	● ● ● ● ●
OUTLOOK	● ● ● ● ●

Tiffany, Gallé, & Followers

ONE MAN WHO BROUGHT unabashed luxury into 20th century life was Louis Comfort Tiffany, an American with a highly developed taste for the exotic. In 1880 he was invited to redecorate parts of the White House, and from there his firm, LCT and Associated Artists, went from strength to strength.

He conceived on a grand scale, and glassware formed only a part of his vast decorative schemes, but it is much coveted because of its unparalleled beauty and originality. His "Favrile" glass, which means glass made by hand, is among the most sought-after glass today.

When making vessels, he sought asymmetry, and he collaborated with Arthur Nash to produce pitted finishes that resembled the Antique glass he had seen during his tours of Europe. An example of this was his "Cypriote" glass and "Lava" glass. Tiffany never forgot he was designing for the new rich of the U.S., and in search of the luxury look he sometimes used real gold pieces as the basis of his decorations.

Perhaps the most beautiful objects made under his name are the table lamps which received international acclaim in 1900 when the "Dragonfly" lamp designed by Clara Driscoll was exhibited in Paris. For beauty it was closely rivalled by the famous "Wistaria" lamp, designed by Mrs. Curtis Freschel, also in 1900.

Douglas Nash continued to make glass in the Tiffany style in the 1920s, and Tiffany's firm had many other imitators, especially in America, among them Handel and Co. and the Quezal Glass and Decorating Company.

One of the pioneers of new glass was Emile Gallé, the founder of the Nancy school of glassmaking, who was born in 1846 and trained as a ceramicist. As a designer, he was mainly influenced by Japanese art, which had made its first appearance in Paris in the 1860s and was enhanced in Gallé's case by his friendship with a Japanese botanist who was a student at the Ecole Forestière in Nancy.

Gallé is famous for his soft-colored vases decorated with flowers and foliage, the design etched onto pale blue or amber-tinted glass. He also made "pâte de verre" and "clair de lune" glass, which had a translucent glow like moonlight, as well as the very difficult to achieve "marqueterie de verre," in which colored pieces were pressed into semi-molten glass before it cooled. He signed all his pieces and, after he died in 1904, his factory continued in operation under his friend and assistant Victor Prouve until 1931. After his death a star was added to the mark "Gallé" on the factory's pieces.

There are many imitators of Gallé, among whom were the Muller brothers of Luneville; Auguste Legras of Le Verre Français in Paris; Schneider Cristalleria of Epinay-sur-Seine whose rarest pieces are signed "Carder." Perhaps the greatest,

ABOVE *In his Jack-in-the-Pulpit vases, Tiffany found the ideal shape with which to display his iridescent glass. Peacock blue was one of his most successful colors.*

COST	● ● ● ● ●
OUTLOOK	● ● ● ● ●

ABOVE *Mold-blown glass vase double overlaid with a design of elephants. Gallé was widely imitated but few could match his skill and artistry.*

COST	● ● ● ● ●
OUTLOOK	● ● ● ● ●

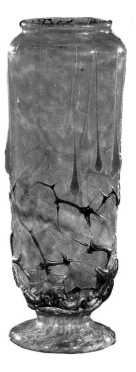

ABOVE *Glass vase internally decorated in bold style by Cristalleries Daum, France.*

COST	● ● ● ● ●
OUTLOOK	● ● ● ●

ABOVE CENTER *Yellow Daum vases. Daum work shows high artistic standards though frequently compared unfavorably with Gallé.*

COST	● ● ● ●
OUTLOOK	● ● ● ●

ABOVE *Crown of Thorns vase of deep pink shading to amber glass by Cristalleries Daum. 1911.*

COST	● ● ● ●
OUTLOOK	● ● ● ●

LEFT *Tiffany flower-form vases in Favrile glass; they made him world-famous at the Art Nouveau Exhibition, Paris, 1900.*

COST	● ● ● ● ●
OUTLOOK	● ● ● ● ●

however, were the Daum brothers, August and Jean, who started the Cristalleries de Nancy, which, like Schneider's *cristallerie,* has continued to the present day and has always been in the top rank of glass manufacturers. The brothers are particularly famous for their bulbous-shaped Art Nouveau lamps of colored glass with enameled decorations and hydrochloric acid etching. Among the artists who worked for Daum was Salvador Dali.

American Glass

OPALESCENT GLASS HAS BEEN one of the great favorites of the 20th century for collectors and artists alike. Tiffany and Gallé were impressed by the sheen that could be found on antique pieces of glass and though opal glass could be made quite easily, the multicolored beauty of true opalescent glass was due to the work of an American artist of French descent named John La Farge (1835-1910). He developed the technique of refining this glass to the point where it was possible to eliminate the need for overlaid paint.

La Farge was only one of the artists and craftsmen working in glass in America during the 20th century, and it is a most varied field for collecting. There are figurines, doorknobs, tableware, bottles, jars, toys, lamps, and paperweights from which to choose, not to mention the glass containers which once contained whisky, gin, medicine, perfume, or even milk or pickles.

Some present-day bottle making plants in the U.S., such as the Owens-Illinois plant at Glassboro, New Jersey, have their origins back in the 18th century. Bottle collecting is particularly interesting because retailers were anxious to have easily recognized containers with an individual "identity" for their products. The waisted Coca Cola bottle, a classic of its kind, is a case in point. This style of bottle only made its appearance after about 1916. Before that, from 1886 onward, Coca Cola was sold in cylindrical bottles with sloping shoulders which are now sought after by bottle collectors. A bottle with its name embossed in red or yellow dates after 1933.

Other pieces of American glass to look out for include the products of the Akro Agate company of Clarksburg, West Virginia, which was founded around 1911 and originally manufactured children's marbles and games. By 1920 it had captured most of the marbles' market for America and in 1935 the company branched out into other products including children's toys, particularly brightly colored tea sets which are collectors' items today.

Look out too for the glass known as Depression glass, which was machine pressed and cheaply produced in vast quantities in the 1920s and 1930s. It appears as candlesticks, coasters, ashtrays, cups and saucers, tea services and salt and pepper sets. Another modern favorite is Carnival glass, so named because it used to be given away as prizes at side shows. It is pressed glass which was sprayed with different colors on the interior instead of the exterior and this produced an iridescent effect.

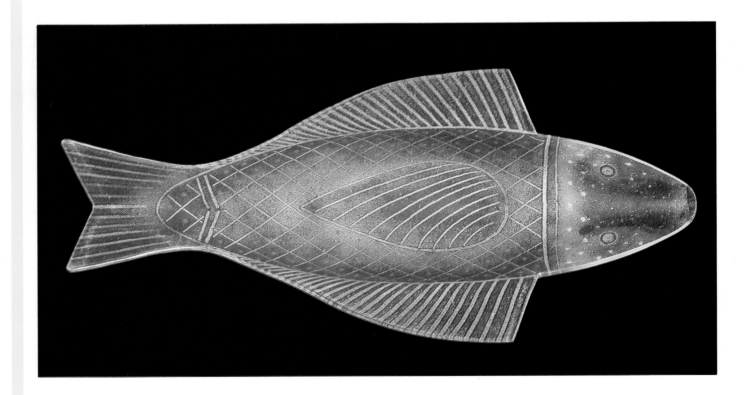

BELOW *Colorless lead glass cut and engraved vase from Haselbauer & Sons, c. 1911-1920.*

| COST | ● ● ● |
| OUTLOOK | ● ● ● |

OPPOSITE PAGE *Fish bowl of kiln-formed glass, with powdered glass enamel decoration, by Maurice Heaton, c. 1955.*

| COST | ● ● ● |
| OUTLOOK | ● ● ● |

RIGHT *Steuben Glass, 1920s.*

| COST | ● ● ● |
| OUTLOOK | ● ● ● |

BELOW *Depression glass tableware with a Florentine pattern, 1934-37.*

| COST | ● ● ● |
| OUTLOOK | ● ● ● |

ABOVE *Effective black and silver engraved bowl by Steuben Glass, 1929.*

| COST | ● ● ● |
| OUTLOOK | ● ● ● |

Scandinavian Glass

THE GLASSWARE FOUND in most modern homes today derives its inspiration from designs pioneered in Scandinavia and Finland. The keynote of work done by designers in those countries was simplicity and practicality combined with good design. Today's Conran's glass can trace its descent straight back to Finland.

At the beginning of the century, the glassmaking industry was thriving in Finland. Architect Alvar Aalto designed asymmetrical vases in clear green glass for the Iittala Glass Works; Arttu Brummer, Director of the School of Arts and Crafts in Helsinki, designed for the Riihimaki Glass Works, and Timo Sarpanevo also worked for Iittala. Their work was copied by young glass workers all over Europe.

After World War I, Sweden took up the lead in glass-making in Northern Europe and the Orrefors Glass Works reached its peak. It specialized in well-designed glass for everyday use. Its "Graal" vases, developed in 1916 by Simon Gate, are still being made. A notable recent example was the Graal bowl by Eva Englund. The name "Graal" derives from "Holy Grail," and the clear glass bowls, often very heavy, were fluidly decorated with cut and etched patterns.

Edvin Ohstrom worked at Orrefors from 1936 and developed "Ariel" glass with its embedded air bubbles which also started a new trend. Gunnar Cyren developed "Pop Age" glasses with bands of different colors. Other Swedish firms were Kosta, which made cut glass and tableware, and Boda, which produced glass in very progressive designs and which merged with Kosta in 1970. In Denmark a famous glassmaker is Jacob Bang who still works at Holmegaard Glassverk.

BELOW CENTER *Colorless Iittala glass dish with characteristically strong, bold shape, by Tapio Wirkkala, Finland, c. 1952.*

| COST | ● ● ● |
| OUTLOOK | ● ● ● |

BELOW *Orrefors "Ariel" vase designed by Ingeborg Lundir of Sweden.*

| COST | ● ● ● |
| OUTLOOK | ● ● ● |

BELOW *The cool, clean lines of Scandinavian glass appealed to the postwar generation. This vase of colorless glass encasing aqua blue is by Jacob Bang of Denmark, c. 1959.*

| COST | ● ● ● |
| OUTLOOK | ● ● ● |

ABOVE *Leading architect and designer Alvar Aalto set the style of asymmetrical vases in clear glass with designs such as these from the late 1930s.*

COST	● ● ●	
OUTLOOK	● ● ● ●	

RIGHT *Group of two-color vases designed by Timo Sarpanevo for the Karhula Iittala glassworks in Finland.*

COST	● ● ●
OUTLOOK	● ● ●

Glasses & Bottles

IN THE 19TH CENTURY people drank from deeply engraved glasses, often colored ruby-red, that felt heavy to the hand, but glass tableware was to experience a metamorphosis, especially through the products of the Whitefriars-based firm of James Powell & Sons, which produced glass to the designs of William Morris and Philip Webb. Their artistic director Harry J. Powell contributed much to the development of modern glass in England by producing hand-blown glass in Roman styles.

In Europe, the change was even more radical. Koloman Moser designed colored and irridescent wine glasses. Josef Hoffmann, who died in 1955, was a Vienna Secessionist architect who produced the Broncit range of glassware, with elegant black and white decorations around the bowls of the wine glasses. These were produced by Lobmeyr of Vienna who also made drinking glasses designed by Adolf Loos. In Holland in the 1930s some beautiful glass, including elegant drinking glasses, was produced at Leerdam Glass Works, particularly to designs by Andreas Copier. Finnish and Swedish glassmakers continue to lead the field in producing glasses that feel good in the hand and look well to the eye.

The sparse symmetry of Scandinavian glassware is in contrast to the more baroque designs still being produced in Murano, the center of the Venetian glassmaking industry. The small island three miles from Venice, known as Murano, has been the site of the Venetian glass industry since the 12th century, when glassmakers were ordered out of the city Venice itself because of the danger of fire from their furnaces. Some families have been engaged in glassmaking in Murano for centuries.

In Britain one of the centers of domestic glassmaking is Stourbridge where the firm of Stuart and Sons still operates. They have employed many original designers including Eric Ravillious and G. John Luxton. Irish glassware is also notable because it alone still reproduces some 19th-century styles in its elegant, deeply cut goblets and decanters. Waterford Glass closed down in the 1850s after producing table glass for over 70 years, but reopened in 1949 to make reproductions of pieces produced from the 18th to the mid-19th century. Their speciality is flint glass tableware, elaborately cut and reflecting light from the hundreds of points on the deeply etched surfaces.

People who appreciate a good wine glass should seek out attractive examples from modern makers like Dartington which specialize in tableware with clean, elegant lines, and Thomas Webb which is still producing its fine crystal. Wedgwood Glass Ware, which has factories at King's Lynn and Galway, Ireland, makes drinking glasses, decanters, and

ABOVE *Colorless lead goblet and champagne glass are cut and engraved to show off the color of the wine in this 1950s "Eden" pattern from Stourbridge, England.*

| COST | ● ● |
| OUTLOOK | ● ● ● |

OPPOSITE TOP *Laurence Whistler stipple-engraved glass, entitled "The Overflowing Landscape."*

| COST | ● ● ● |
| OUTLOOK | ● ● ● ● |

OPPOSITE BELOW *Wine glasses of the 1920s, with cut and engraved decorations on crystal and on ruby and black cased over crystal, from Steuben Glass, United States.*

| COST | ● ● |
| OUTLOOK | ● ● ● |

BELOW *Blown glass goblet from Murano, Italy, c. 1935.*

| COST | ● ● ● |
| OUTLOOK | ● ● ● |

Bottles

A hobby far more profitable than the highly speculative one of panning for gold has been growing steadily in the past few years — that of literally digging up the rubbish of yesteryear.

It is said that over three million dollars' worth of relics are being unearthed each year, mostly in the form of bottles which have a ready market in both Britain and the U.S. Bottles most popular with collectors fall into four categories:

1. Mineral water, beer, and other beverage bottles.
2. Quack medicine and "Cure-All" bottles.
3. Glass and stone ink bottles.
4. Poison bottles.

One of the rarest poison bottles known is a Binoculars Poison, so called because of its shape. An ice-blue bottle with "Poison" embossed across the shoulder and on each cylinder, it is also embossed "O'Reilly's Patent 1905" on the base. Dig one of these up and you are talking about $1300 plus.

paperweights. Studio glassmaking, like studio potting, engages the talents of many skilled practitioners of the art and they can be found all over Europe and America.

Wine glass collectors are also interested in the work of artists like Laurence Whistler, who engraved designs of imaginative landscapes onto shapes by Whitefriars, Leerdam, or Steuben. In galleries and art colleges, interesting work is to be found by young engravers who will no doubt be collectors' favorites in years to come.

Stained Glass

ABOVE *Leaded stained glass panel by George Walton after a design by C.R. Mackintosh.*

COST	● ● ● ● ●
OUTLOOK	● ● ● ●

BELOW *Art Nouveau stained glass.*

COST	● ● ● ● ●
OUTLOOK	● ● ● ● ●

ALPHONSE MUCHA IS USUALLY categorized as the creator of the ubiquitous Art Nouveau posters. The romantic, flowing-haired ladies with their elegant profiles were not his only memorable achievement, however, because Mucha, who is known as the High Priest of the Art Nouveau movement and whose career burgeoned around the turn of the 20th century, created one of the most superb pieces of stained glass in the world — a magnificent, brilliantly colored window which can still be seen in Prague Cathedral, having, by some miracle, survived the ravages of war.

The example he set in seeing the artistic possibilities of stained glass was eagerly taken up by other artists of the period until the end of the 1930s. Stained glass was not only used for windows and door panels, in which form it decorated everything from small suburban houses to stately mansions, but it was also made into ornamental pieces and insets for furniture. Collectors with a discriminating eye used to search sites scheduled for demolition to rescue bits of stained glass, but in recent years these treasures are harder to find.

Charles Rennie Mackintosh made clever use of stained glass to highlight his elegant furniture; in America, John La Farge and Louis Comfort Tiffany seized on its possibility for decorative pieces; it was even used in the manufacture of Art Nouveau jewelry. Tiffany in particular was commissioned to execute stained glass windows for the new large houses springing up all over America and he devised a style based on Japanese influences which he later used in the creation of his magnificent table lamps. He often depicted flowers — cherry blossom, water lilies, wisteria, reeds, and poppies — in his themes. Tiffany pieces bring some astonishing prices when they turn up for sale.

Stained-glass windows in churches have been traditional since the Middle Ages, but received a huge boost in the mid-20th century because of the desire to record survivors' thanks after the holocaust of two world wars. The work of artists commissioned to create those memorial windows marked a breakthrough in the technology of stained glass because they were able to cast aside the old convention in which the lead separating the pieces of glass was treated as a kind of barrier. For modern artists it became a flowing line and a way of illustrating the theme.

ABOVE *Lighting panel designed for elevators of the Daily News Building in New York, 1930s.*

COST	● ● ● ●
OUTLOOK	● ● ● ●

BELOW *Early 1900s "Tree of Life" door in leaded glass by Frank Lloyd Wright.*

COST	● ● ● ● ●
OUTLOOK	● ● ● ●

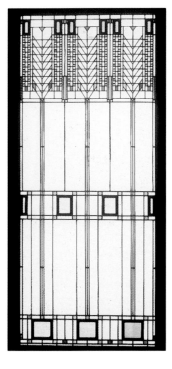

LEFT *Turn-of-the-century landscape window glowing with rich color, by L.C. Tiffany.*

COST	● ● ● ● ●
OUTLOOK	● ● ● ●

BELOW *Pair of stained glass windows depicting Beatrice and Dante by William Willett, c. 1910-20.*

COST	● ● ● ●
OUTLOOK	● ● ●

Chair by C.R. Mackintosh.

CHAPTER THREE

Furniture

INTERIORS

BEDS & SOFAS

SCREENS

TABLES

CHAIRS

CABINETS

Introduction

Turn-of-the-century veneered walnut desk by Emile Gallé.

AT THE BEGINNING of the century, furniture was manufactured for the upper classes and the prosperous middle class who had money to spend because of industrial expansion. They could afford to patronize artisans and artists such as those who gathered around William Morris in Britain, Louis Majorelle in France, or Gustav Stickley in the United States. There was never a better time for designers to put their ideas into effect. It is noticeable that many of the best-known designers were architects who wanted to set their personal seal not only on the houses they built but on everything that was inside them as well. They were polymaths.

It did not take long, however, for the rejection of machinery to be seen as pompous by people who were thrilled at the new advances they saw around them. Automobiles revolutionized transportation, electricity lit up streets and houses, and artists reveled in the opportunities that modern methods offered them. The Bauhaus Group and Charles Rennie Mackintosh's contemporaries still wanted to design entire "living schemes" but they were also prepared to work for and with commerce.

Until the 1930s furniture design continued to go hand in hand with architectural commissions for the rich, and there was intense activity. The 1929 crash and the Great Depression of 1929 brought this Golden Age to a halt. Without patrons designers could no longer work, and furniture makers had to look to a new market, which they found among the suburban dwellers in the new respectable, middle-class houses that were springing up around every town and city. These buyers did not want Bugatti's eccentric chairs or Paul Iribe's sharkskin-topped tables; they wanted three-piece suites and well-made wardrobes, and that was what they got.

A survey of furniture making over the first 80 years of the 20th century shows it broken sharply into two parts — the Age of Luxury and the Age of Practicality. However, even in the practical period, attractive items were being made and craftsmen continued to take a pride in their work though the heady days were over.

Side table with mirror in silvered and painted wood with chromium plating; by Kem Weber, 1928-9.

Strongly geometrical six-sided table by Josef Hoffmann, Vienna, 1904.

Walnut fishing tackle cabinet with barber pole inlay; Ernest Gimson, 1913.

Elegant bureau à cylindre in ebony and ivory from Rulhmann, 1923.

Dressing table, stool, and mirror designed in the 1930s by American Paul Frankl.

Chaise longue by Le Corbusier, introducing modern lines in 1928.

Boldly Sixties designer-look Egg Chair by Jacobsen, 1968.

Inlaid round table commissioned by Renate John from The David Linley Company in the 1980s.

Reclining chair that offers the right support for relaxing; by Kjaerholm, 1968.

Interiors

WILLIAM MORRIS AND the Arts and Crafts movement stressed the value of craftsmanship but artisans could not afford these pieces that were never cheap. Yet the styles Morris and his followers made popular were copied by hundreds of other furniture makers and a little of the Arts and Crafts' ideal permeated into ordinary homes. Cottage-type furniture was very popular.

Some important designers whose work contributed to the domestic ambience throughout the years include Ernest Gimson; Ambrose Heal, who established the famous London furniture store; Betty Joel, whose furniture showed the many effects that could be achieved with wood; and Gordon Russell who set up a factory making furniture in the best craftsmanship tradition at Broadway, Worcester. Their mantles have been taken over by recent designers such as Terence Conran and Laura Ashley, who have had great success and considerable influence on the way we live now.

Architects also had a big influence because the homes they designed cried out to be furnished in a new and original way. Model railway tycoon W. Basset Lowke employed Charles Rennie Mackintosh to design his house and to suggest how it should look inside. Peter Behrens, a German architect of the 1920s, and his compatriot and fellow architect Walter Gropius, a refugee from the Nazis and principal of the Bauhaus, made the streamlined look fashionable.

BELOW *Living room furniture by Conran had strong appeal in the 1960s for its young, contemporary styling and contrast with the designs and colors of the past.*

COST	● ●
OUTLOOK	● ● ●

LEFT *Eileen Gray furniture from the 1920s.*

COST	● ● ● ●
OUTLOOK	● ● ●

RIGHT *Scandinavian interior design from 1957: furniture by Federico Fogh and Inger Klingenberg.*

COST	● ● ●
OUTLOOK	● ● ●

BELOW *A post-Modern interior designed by Memphis, blending Pop-art, classicism, and Art Deco.*

COST	● ● ● ●
OUTLOOK	● ● ● ● ●

Beds & Sofas

"AND SO TO BED," sighed Samuel Pepys with a note of pleasant anticipation. Because people spend one-third of their lives asleep, there has always been a great interest in the designing of beds.

The 20th century saw the change from mattresses filled with feathers and set on metal springs to the inlaid box mattress on which most people now sleep. The shape of beds changed too, and there has been a move away from the imposing beds popular in the 19th century and after, first to the slimmed-down single beds that were the rage in the 1930s and then back to more companionable double, or even king-sized beds. The 1950s saw the advent of the reproduction brass bed and since then the fourposter has made a comeback.

Furniture designers translated the trends of their times into the shape of their beds. Early 20th-century bedframes were made from heavy wood, often highly polished walnut, or from Arts and Crafts dark stained wood with inlet cuts. Until the 1940s they usually had head- and footboards but the footboard has since disappeared.

Some of the prettiest beds to look out for in furniture auctions are the glossy white painted beds with endboards carved with posies of flowers. In the 1930s there was also a craze for Chinese style furniture; bedroom suites were produced painted in light colors with sprays of flowers and exotic birds decorating the surfaces. Suites of this type could be picked up for around $100 a few years ago; now you would have to multiply that by twenty.

Another highly desirable bed from the past is the bergère bed. This type was often imported from France, it had double cane head- and footboards and a heavily carved outer frame. Bergère was also popular for sofas and side chairs. The double cane form of construction is the best and most expensive. When bergère suites come up for sale there is usually keen competition to buy provided the cane is not too damaged.

Modern furniture designers have seized on the sofa as the ideal means of expressing the flowing lines which they admire. Earlier Arts and Crafts furniture makers built cottage-type sofas with wooden slatted backs, descendants of the old English wooden benchlike settles. These proved popular with buyers, especially because they were space saving; they were given a utilitarian function by having a hinged box for storing blankets as the seat.

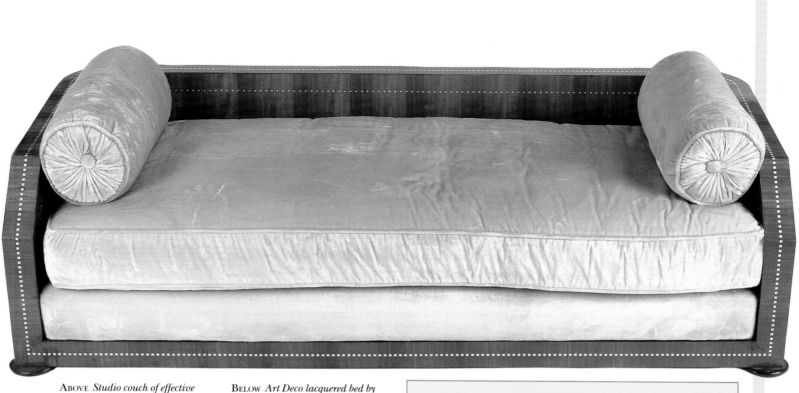

ABOVE *Studio couch of effective design.*

COST	● ●	
OUTLOOK	● ●	

OPPOSITE LEFT *This exotic ebène de macassar and bird's-eye maple couch, upholstered in zebra skin, is in the style of Jules Leleu.*

COST	● ● ●	
OUTLOOK	● ●	

BELOW *Art Deco lacquered bed by Jean Dunand, who designed furnishings for the great ocean liners.*

COST	● ● ● ●
OUTLOOK	● ● ●

Betty Joel

Betty Joel is best known for her simple, unpretentious pieces of furniture designed for the smaller house or apartment and her clever use of unusual woods such as laurel, greywood, sycamore, Queensland walnut, and bird's-eye maple.

She founded Betty Joel Ltd in 1919 and successfully exhibited at the Exhibition of British Industrial Art in 1933, supplying the Russell Workshops with designs from 1934 before retiring in 1937. Most of the pieces are marked with the date and signature.

Screens

SCREENS WERE ESSENTIAL in drafty homes with winds whistling under the doors and down the immense chimneys. They were propped around armchairs as a kind of windbreak but it was only when a certain sophistication entered home design that what was on the screen became important.

Some of the most beautiful screens to be found today are those that were imported from China and Japan from the 18th century onward. Often made of lacquer and painted with supreme artistry, these fetch high prices. Some of them had as many as six or eight wings, though the three- or four-winged screen is the commonest.

Screen makers working at home often used leather for the wings of their screens, and in a few cases these can be found painted with Chinese themes in imitation of the imported ones. Other screens carried hunting patterns to match the tapestries that hung on castle walls.

As comfort in the home increased, the need for screens diminished. In the 19th century they were more and more regarded as decorative objects. Some were made half size and were delicate with gold lacquer frames and cloth-covered or canework wings. Others, bigger and more robust, were kept for their heat-retaining function and it was a common nursery pursuit to paste them all over with the brilliantly colored scraps popular at that time. Scrap-covered screens frequently turn up at auction.

The Edwardians developed screens into sophisticated accessories, using them in the bedroom as a shield behind which to dress, particularly in actors' and actresses' dressing rooms. They are still bought as furnishing for the bedroom and are used to display brightly colored shawls.

The decorative function of the screen was seized on by the avant-garde designers of the 1920s who treated them like canvases. Commissions were undertaken to decorate screens to fit in with room layouts. There are some magnificent 1920s screens to be seen — but only bought at vast expense. The Parisian artist André Mare made a fabulous one in lacquer over parchment with bronze frames and feet. It was brilliantly colored and based on the paintings of Gauguin. People with shallower pockets might look out for other 1920s screens made of cloth and designed in geometric patterns.

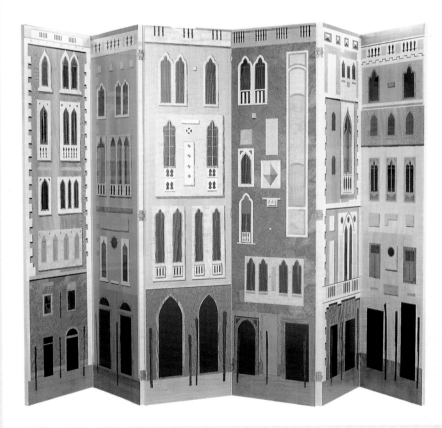

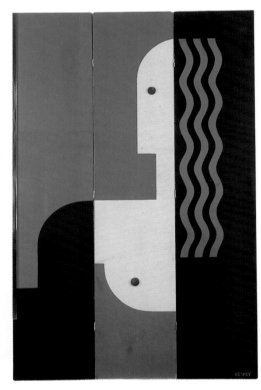

OPPOSITE LEFT *Venetian screen by The David Linley Company, c. 1980.*

| COST | ● ● ● ● |
| OUTLOOK | ● ● ● ● |

OPPOSITE RIGHT *"Lysistrata" screen of lacquered wood and chrome by Donald Deskey, c. 1930.*

| COST | ● ● ● |
| OUTLOOK | ● ● ● |

BELOW *Screen of inlaid woods showing animal scenes, by Frank Brangwyn for Rowley Galleries, c. 1920.*

| COST | ● ● ● ● |
| OUTLOOK | ● ● ● ● |

Carlo Bugatti

Carlo Bugatti was a furniture designer of genius who does not fit into any of the known categories or movements. Born in Milan in 1855, he lived until 1940, and the designs he produced for furniture are frequently bizarre but always stimulating and attractive. He used asymmetrical uprights on his chairs, painted vellum, pewter, tassels, fringes, stamped brass, and circlets of wood carved to look like native African art. Some of his pieces have a distinct "jungle" look and are so original that even the pieces he did not sign are easily recognizable.

Tables

BELOW *Macmurdo writing desk
with characteristically straight
Edwardian lines.*

COST	● ● ●
OUTLOOK	● ● ● ●

THE GREATEST ARCHITECTS of the early 20th century were also
furniture designers because they wanted their houses to be
equipped with the sort of things which would suit the new,
revolutionary lines. The shape of a table is ideal for expressing
new ideas; tables can be flowing, rigid, geometric, or
eccentric and the period under review shows every possible
variation on the theme.

The French designer Hector Guimard (1867-1942) was
one of the foremost creators of the flowing style, using plant
patterns as the theme. He shared this style with Louis Majorelle and E. Vallin, who both belonged to the school of Nancy
and used local woods in their furniture. They carried the
fluidity of wood to its highest expression.

Working at the same time were the Arts and Crafts disciples who preferred their tables to be stark and plain, modeled
on the long table of the Old English hall. Again, however, the
emphasis was on craftsmanship, though of a different, more
artisan kind. The solid, round-legged dining tables found in
many 1930s homes were direct descendants of the Arts and
Crafts tables, specially designed to fit into smaller homes,
with drop sides or extending wings.

It was another architect, Charles Rennie Mackintosh, who
provided a link between those two schools of design. He drew
on the flowing flower and plant theme but he also admired
the starkness and simplicity of the Arts and Crafts school, so
his furniture, designed in harmony with his elegant buildings, was spare and slim, elongated in line but clearly modeled on natural forms. His tables particularly returned to the
Anglo-Saxon tradition of simplicity and solidity. In some of
them the vertical lines were multiplied to suggest a forest of
tall stems.

The link between Mackintosh and later designers is also
clearly discernible. Designers like Clément Rousseau, who
was working in the 1920s, made furniture from rare woods
and embellished pieces with sharkskin. His banner was taken
up by Bugatti whose furniture was richly decorated with
brass, copper, leather, beading, and thongs. His work is currently enjoying a great vogue after making splendid prices in
Sotheby's sale of the rock musician Elton John's collection in
1988.

Other trendsetting tables were designed by Mies van der
Rohe and Marcel Breuer whose dining-room furniture,
made in the 1920s, is still modern and sought after today. It
was Mies van der Rohe who pioneered the use of nickel-
plated tubing and black lacquered wood.

ABOVE *Writing desk, designed by
C.F.A. Voysey and made in England
by W.H. Tingey in 1896.*

COST	● ● ●
OUTLOOK	● ● ●

BELOW *Oak table with brass fittings
from the early 1900s by Josef
Hoffmann.*

COST	● ● ●
OUTLOOK	● ● ●

RIGHT *Writing table and chair in oak and shagreen by Jean-Michel Frank, 1928.*

COST	● ● ●
OUTLOOK	● ● ● ●

BELOW *Late 1920s coffee table with brushed nickel base and Bakelite top by Donald Deskey.*

COST	● ● ●
OUTLOOK	● ● ● ●

Chairs

A STUDY OF THE chair through the 20th century gives a graphic illustration of the development of furniture design.

Furniture designers tended to belong to one of two schools. There was the William Morris Arts and Crafts school, whose ideas were taken to America by Englishman Charles Lock Eastlake. It preferred rustic-style furniture and its chairs were sturdy, solid-legged, often with thonged leather seats. The second school, which dominated European design, preferred the Art Nouveau style in which wood was treated as a fluid medium, and the chairs designed by Émile Gallé and Louis Majorelle had a flowing, almost plastic, appearance.

Both schools went in for added decorations. Arts and Crafts furniture was embossed with bronze or copper, studded with colored stones or painted. Art Nouveau designs often featured intricate marquetry work and curvilinear carving.

It was the genius of Charles Rennie Mackintosh that took ideas from both of these schools and developed them to their ultimate expression, producing elegantly attenuated chairs

with just enough curve to make the outline interesting.

The ideas of Gerrit Rietveld, however, burst upon designers like a bombshell and inspired a new generation in the world of furniture design — men like Marcel Breuer of the Bauhaus, who produced his Wassily Chair in tubular steel and leather; Mies van der Rohe of the MR and Brno chairs; and Finnish designer Alvar Aalto, who produced chairs in his firm Artex in the 1930s.

The advent of plastics during World War II brought a new material to the notice of chair manufacturers, and Charles Eames's glass fiber Dax Chair, Eero Saarinen's plastic Tulip Chair, and Carl Jacobs' plastic stacking chairs, found today all over the world, were the results.

Postwar Italians were particularly keen on good chair design, and among notable makers were Joe Colombo, Sergio Mazza, and Mario Bellini.

Fortunately for chair buyers, they believed that as well as being visually attractive, a chair should be comfortable. Rietveld's ideal of keeping a sitter alert has been abandoned.

LEFT *Oak chair designed by C.F.A. Voysey, c. 1909.*

| COST | ● ● ● | |
| OUTLOOK | ● ● ● ● | |

CENTER *Wassily chair, 1925 — the first to be made of tubular steel.*

| COST | ● ● ● | |
| OUTLOOK | ● ● ● | |

OPPOSITE ABOVE *Plastic chair by Eero Saarinen, 1957.*

| COST | ● ● ● | |
| OUTLOOK | ● ● ● | |

RIGHT *One of a set of six Wiener Werkstatte black stained lime oak dining chairs by Josef Hoffmann.*

| COST | ● ● ● ● | |
| OUTLOOK | ● ● ● ● | |

Charles Rennie Mackintosh

Charles Rennie Mackintosh (1868-1928) is one of Glasgow's most famous sons. An architectural student who attended night classes at Glasgow School of Art, he was to become one of the most influential designers of the 20th century, tackling everything from buildings and furnishing to the electroplated teaspoons for Miss Cranston's restaurants in Glasgow.

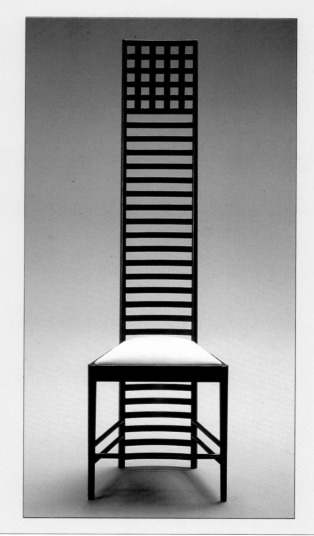

Gerrit Rietveld

The most significant chair of the 20th century was Gerrit Rietveld's Red Blue Chair, made in 1918. It embodied all the ideas of Rietveld and his friends whose theories were set out in *Der Stijl* magazine. They believed that design should express structure uncluttered by ornaments, and they used primary colors and black to great effect. Rietveld's chair stands at the head of the line of 20th-century "modern" chairs.

Cabinets

THE WORD "CABINET" derives from the Italian *gabinetto* meaning a closet, a press, or a chest of drawers. As pieces of furniture, cabinets had their British beginnings in the 17th century when they were designed either for specialized storage or display. They were generally imported from Europe as possessions for the rich who used them to display collections of fossils, shells, minerals, or coins. It was not until the 18th and 19th centuries that British craftsmen turned their hands to creating cabinets. The styles they adopted at that time, such as glass-fronted Sheraton or Adam style cabinets, are still being copied and continue to be popular.

The Edwardians loved cabinets and there are many examples of fine, inlaid, glass-fronted display ones still to be bought, though prices have escalated over the past decade. The drawback is generally size because they are usually 5ft (1.5 meters) wide, making them awkward in small rooms. A more manageable type is a smaller display cabinet on spindly legs; again there are fine Edwardian examples about.

Throughout the century furniture makers stuck faithfully to the glass-fronted cabinet as a suitable piece of living-room equipment. In houses both grand and humble, they were used to display wedding china and any cherished pieces of glass or pottery that a family possessed. These cabinets were still being produced in various forms and large numbers until the 1950s, but since then they have tended to be displaced by the modern "wall units" or room dividers with open shelves for display. More basic cabinets were designed for the kitchen, sometimes with glazed doors but more commonly with open shelves. Those made of pine are especially sought after by collectors.

The Jazz Age saw the advent of the cocktail cabinet which opened up to reveal an array of glinting glasses and gleaming shakers, ice tongs and other pieces of equipment for making cocktails. Some of these cabinets were lined with tinted mirrors and a few played tunes when opened. These are bound to become collectors' treasures.

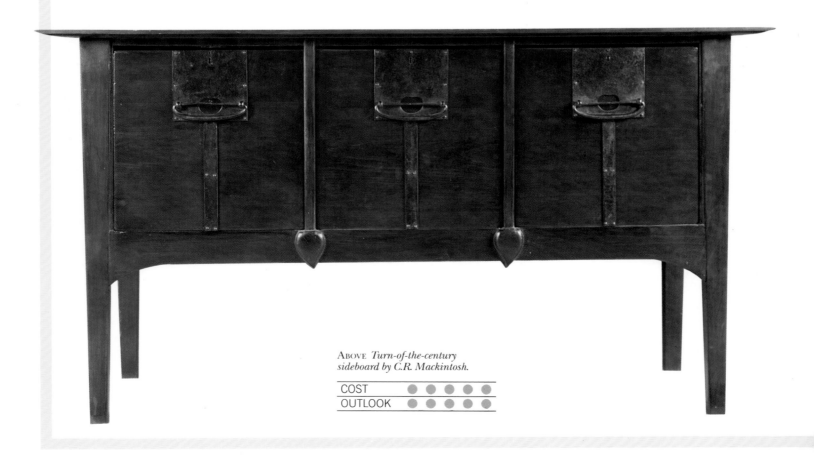

ABOVE *Turn-of-the-century sideboard by C.R. Mackintosh.*

COST	● ● ● ● ○
OUTLOOK	● ● ● ● ●

LEFT *Cabinet from a suite by Hector Guimard, 1900.*

ABOVE *Art Deco cocktail cart with glass panels by Lalique.*

COST	● ● ● ● ●
OUTLOOK	● ● ● ● ●

COST	● ● ● ● ●
OUTLOOK	● ● ● ● ●

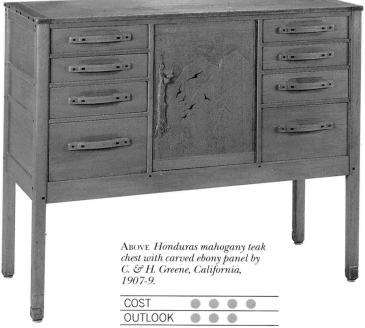

ABOVE *Honduras mahogany teak chest with carved ebony panel by C. & H. Greene, California, 1907-9.*

COST	● ● ● ●
OUTLOOK	● ● ●

*Wall-light of silver-painted wrought
iron with glass shade by Edgar-
William Brandt.*

CHAPTER FOUR

Furnishings

WALLPAPERS & TEXTILES

SOFT FURNISHINGS

WROUGHT IRON

LIGHTING

Introduction

THE THINGS THAT people own in their homes tell historians a great deal about them and the time in which they live. Twentieth-century homemakers set out to create a deliberate contrast to the claustrophobic home life of their parents and grandparents. Windows were opened and light came in; colors were fresher; over-ornate decoration and table-leg frills disappeared. The pared-down vision of Charles Rennie Mackintosh pervaded many aspects of design. Speed, as exemplified by the automobile, was the popular god.

At the same time industry was expanding and creating markets. Wants were created in order to be assuaged. Everyone wanted "modernity" and, with its advance, home interiors changed. Gas lighting gave way to electricity; magazines and newspapers were accessible to all classes of society, and through advertisements people's ambitions were changed. The fear of being out-of-fashion gripped those whose families had never bothered about such things before, partly because they had not heard of fashion and partly because they could not have afforded to keep up with it. Even during the Depression, ordinary people wanted possessions more than at any time in the past, and when the slump was over, a general sense of euphoria brought about a spending spree that encompassed rugs on the floor and gnomes in the garden.

Mass production also brought new things within the reach of the working classes. No longer was home furnishing a luxury. Everybody wanted a new lampshade or bright new wallpaper on their walls. The advertising industry, through psychological techniques, created a society that craved possessions. New houses sprang up, each furnished with painted lampshades and pretty bedlinen. The old extended family structure, particularly of the working classes, disappeared and as people strove to beautify their close surroundings, the "nuclear family" was created.

Wisteria table lamp with triple overlay by Gallé, c. 1900.

American World War II "Lone Star" quilt with "prairie point" edging.

Pair of silver candelabra with acrylic stems, by Brian Asquith, 1984.

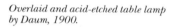

Overlaid and acid-etched table lamp by Daum, 1900.

Carpet design, Radio City Music Hall, New York, c. 1925.

Furnishing fabric by Dufrene of Paris, 1925-30.

Selection of hanging lamps with the look of the 1950s, by Rotaflex.

Pop art furnishing fabric designed by Sue Thatcher for Warner, England, 1969.

Liberty's Chesham II Collection of cotton furnishing fabrics, 1986.

Pair of lamps in blown glass with enameled wood base by Mark McDonnell, United States, 1986.

"Bloomsbury living room" — a Laura Ashley interior.

Wallpapers & Textiles

IN THE LATE Middle Ages, the walls of great houses were covered with tapestries to keep out the cold and introduce color, but people with less money found tapestry buying beyond them, so their walls were either painted or pasted over with colored paper.

When trade began with the East, Chinese wallpapers, beautifully decorated with trees, flowers, and birds, began to be imported but, again, only for the rich.

In the early 19th century new technology made it possible to print rolls of paper on calico printing machines and the wallpaper market expanded enormously. The Victorians loved to cover their walls with paper. It was often dark and gloomy to complement the cluttered rooms, but when William Morris started his innovative design workshop, some of his most popular lines were wallpapers and textiles in fresh, clear, and often colorful patterns.

The "Bird in Thorn Bush" and stylized flower papers done by Morris and Co. and his fellow designers, A.H. Mackmurdo and Charles Annesley Voysey, are still immensely popular. The demand for attractive wallcoverings caused a great expansion in the wallpaper market and Arthur Silver, along with his sons Rex and Harry, opened the Silver Studio which produced over 25,000 different designs for wallpapers and textiles. Rex, who died in 1965, was a particularly talented artist who also produced Silver designs for Liberty & Co. Harold Gilman, a painter of the Camden group at the turn of the century, also designed some attractive papers.

In France the craze was as strong as in England and many Art Nouveau designers had a hand in wallpaper designing, including Georges de Feure who produced papers with intertwining decorations of flowers, birds, and leafy twigs.

As the century progressed, however, the fashion for covering walls with patterns that would detract from the overall design was frowned upon. Architect M.H. Baillie Scott thought that walls should either be left white or stenciled, a fashion that has enjoyed a renaissance recently. Charles Rennie Mackintosh also used stenciling in his room designs, as did Henri van der Velde.

The use of wallpapers, however, never died out completely and during the 1930s and 1940s color and interest in ordinary homes was often provided by wallpaper. Nursery wallpapers were always popular, and Mabel Lucie Attwell and Walter Crane produced designs for them. This fashion has continued with papers featuring Disney characters, Beatrix Potter animals, and characters from television shows like Star Trek.

An interesting collection of wallpapers can be built up and anyone trying their hand at home decorating should never

ABOVE *One of a pair of Arts and Crafts curtains from the early 1900s, the design attributed to Silver Studios.*

COST	● ●
OUTLOOK	● ● ● ●

ABOVE *Wallpaper and fabric design from the* Daily Mail Ideal Home Book *for 1951-2.*

COST	● ●
OUTLOOK	● ● ●

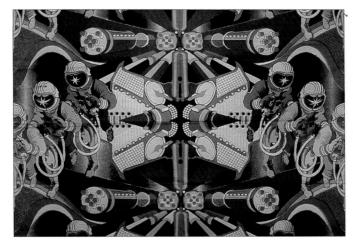

ruthlessly strip a wall without carefully peeling off the layers of old wallpaper first and inspecting them for treasures.

Curtain materials and wall hangings were seen by William Morris as a way of enhancing his decorative schemes and he used the firm of Wardle in Leek, Staffordshire, to print his textiles in the same patterns as the wallpapers.

The textile trade saw in the new craze for home decorating a potential mass market and employed many other artists to produce new designs with the output ranging from cheap cottons to heavy, rich fabrics like those of the Silver Studio.

In the early 20th century, partly because of Morris's advocacy of a return to medieval styles of furnishing and partly because of the impact of the Ballets Russes with their looped swags of brilliantly colored material encasing the stage, there was a renewed craze for wall hangings. Tapestry workshops opened, and one of the first was Edinburgh's Dovecot Tapestry, started in 1912 by the fourth Marquess of Bute. Two master weavers from Morris's studio at Merton Abbey were on the staff. The Dovecot Tapestry is still in existence, weaving a variety of lovely pieces which are collected by connoisseurs all over the world.

Some Bauhaus artists in the 1920s specialized in tapestry making, especially Gunta Stolzl whose work was brilliantly colored and original in style. In Finland, about the same time, peasant rugs became popular for wall hangings and some young designers, including Eva Brummer and Maija Kolsi-Makela, began experimenting with modern fibers and abstract designs. There are still many skilled tapestry makers and much of their work is bought by companies that use it to decorate offices and board rooms. For example, the PepsiCo office in New York has a set of Frank Stella's Had Gadya tapestries proudly on display.

Morris & Co.

In 1861 William Morris, along with other well-known painters, an architect, and an engineer, set up a company whose aims were to produce decorative articles of the very finest quality for "the people." His designs, taken from plant and animal forms, are still very popular today. The company provided, in today's terms, a complete house-furnishing service, supplying everything that could possibly be required within a household, from a stained glass window to a set of teaspoons and such was their success that the firm continued trading until 1940.

To the untrained eye, a bundle of old drapes in a corner of the attic is precisely that, and no more. If, however, they happen to be a pair of wool drapes with matching valance in the "Bird" pattern designed by William Morris, they could be worth about $5000.

Soft Furnishings

THERE IS A strong collecting enthusiasm for 19th-century bed-linen and patchwork quilts, particularly those made in America. By the time the 20th century was under way, the popularity of the sewing machine and the growth of manufacturing industry resulted in less needlework and lacemaking being done at home.

However, if women were not sewing of necessity, they liked to have hobbies and, in the 1930s, sheets of linen, outline-printed with designs of ladies in crinolines and poke bonnets, were sold by the million. All that had to be done was to chain-stitch around the outline, though the more skilled often gave the lady a bouquet of flowers made from French knots. These designs, and other equally simple ones, were made into tablecloths, napkins, guest hand towels, and pictures to hang on the wall. Another favorite hobby was crochet, and skilled practitioners produced tablecloths and dressing-table sets that often turn up now in yard sales.

In the days before nylon, bedlinen was heavy and substantial, and high-quality sheets and pillowcases can be found from the prewar period. Some of the best was made in Northern Ireland, where there was a thriving linen industry. Favorites with collectors are sheets and pillowcases decorated with scallops of flowers and dyed in pale pastel colors. These have a very 1930s look and can still be picked up quite cheaply. The Irish also made beautifully patterned damask tablecloths and napkins, some of them woven with the symbol of the country, the shamrock.

In the 1960s a quilt-making craze spread among middle-class housewives but, on the whole, the making of bedspreads and quilts has been less common during the 20th century. The only exception is the thick quilts that wounded soldiers in World War I made to while away the months, and sometimes years, they had to spend in bed. Some of those rough quilts are mistakenly thought to have been made by the wives of Welsh miners during the General Strike but, in fact, a keen eye can pick out scraps of various army, navy, and flying corps uniform materials in them.

Rugs have not been a major collecting area until recently so there are many good examples to be found in junk stores. At the beginning of the century, rug makers were stuck in traditional styles, and although William Morris translated some of his designs into rugs, they still had a semi-Persian look. It was not until the 1930s that designers began to look at rugs as a new form of artistic expression. Some eye-catching geometric rugs were designed. These have once again come into their own because they fit in well with modern furnishing schemes. One of the major designers was Da Silva Bruhns who designed a range of rugs in beautiful contrasting colors

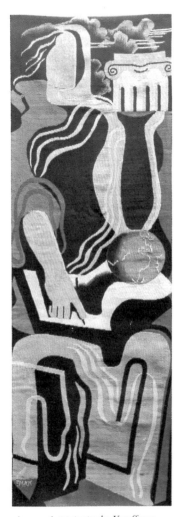

ABOVE *Art tapestry by Kauffer: a new era for artists and for collectors at reasonable prices.*

COST	● ● ●
OUTLOOK	● ● ● ●

ABOVE *English quilt, with Log Cabin pattern, from the 1930s.*

COST	● ● ●
OUTLOOK	● ● ● ●

BELOW *American "double wedding ring" design quilt, c. 1940.*

COST	● ● ●
OUTLOOK	● ● ● ●

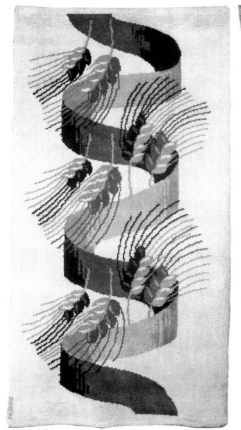

ABOVE *A rug design by Marion Dorn that breaks with traditional patterns.*

COST	● ● ● ●
OUTLOOK	● ● ● ● ●

ABOVE *A modernist hand-knotted wool carpet by Da Silva Bruhns, c. 1930.*

COST	● ● ●
OUTLOOK	● ● ● ●

LEFT *A geometric carpet design by Kauffer.*

COST	● ●
OUTLOOK	● ● ● ●

for the Palace of the Maharajah of Indore between 1930 and 1933. One large rug in fawn, cream, dark brown, and orange was particularly influential, and many manufacturers took up Bruhns's ideas.

Excited by the possibility of rug making, designer Duncan Miller made rectangular rugs woven to look like zebra skins. This was the time when tiger and zebra skins were very popular as floor and bed coverings and his rugs, less prone to damage and more practical, were a huge success.

Modernism affected the output of many traditional rug manufacturers, particularly Templetons, who employed famous designers including Charles Rennie Mackintosh. A rug he designed for them in small squares and rectangles on a ground divided into larger rectangles is now worth a considerable sum of money. Templetons also used designs by Frank Brangwyn, who moved away from geometric themes into more floral swirling styles in pastel greens and pinks.

After World War II much of the output was carpeting for wall-to-wall carpets. A few individual rugs were still made, however, and one of the best from a collecting point of view is a cotton rug woven with a selection of characters from Walt Disney films sold for nurseries and children's bedrooms.

There are still some individual rug makers but the bulk of their output tends to be for tufted wall hangings.

Wrought Iron

PERHAPS THE HIGH POINT of wrought-iron design in the 20th century was reached in the elegant entrances of the Paris Metro stations designed by Hector Guimard. As far as household use is concerned, the use of wrought iron for decorative purposes was popularized in Britain by William Morris. Before his time, wrought iron had been extensively used for railings and decorative gates, but it was the achievement of Morris and his contemporaries to transform it into an art form. They moved away from using straight bar iron to having it hammered out flat and shaped with artistry by skilled artist-blacksmiths. Sometimes they used wrought-iron decorations for pieces of furniture, particularly chests and cabinets.

Architects adopted the medium, and their designs included fluted balconies, wrought-iron panels on doors and windows, and delicately curved and shaped window catches that can still be found at demolition sites today. Architects like Robert Lorimer and Norman Shaw also commissioned blacksmiths to make wrought-iron foot scrapers, andirons, fire baskets, fireplace screens, and lamp brackets to fit in with their decorative schemes.

The architect-designer Christopher Dresser used cast iron when designing hall and umbrella stands in the Gothic style, and these were marked "Coalbrookdale."

Another extensive outlet for wrought iron was garden seats and benches, sometimes with patterns of intertwining fern bracts. These are very valuable today.

In the 1920s the French firm of H. Monand & Cie began making elegant Art Deco marble and wrought-iron radiator covers for the new central heating systems. These were exhibited at the 1925 Paris Exhibition and were extensively copied by other manufacturers.

Up to the present day there has been a school of sculptors executing models and figures in wrought iron, some of them very avant-garde.

BELOW LEFT AND RIGHT *Elevator doors of nickel and brass for The Farmer's Trust Building, 1931 — an example of modern inventions offering the opportunity for modern design.*

COST	● ● ● ●
OUTLOOK	● ● ● ●

Lighting

THE 20TH CENTURY saw not only the introduction of electric lighting but also a revolutionary development in lighting fixtures. The stalactite glass ceiling lamps of Lalique and the triple-tulip standing lamp of Albert Cheuret, along with the beautiful glass lamps created by Daum, Gallé, and their contemporaries, fall into the Art Nouveau period when a significant trend was the use of bronze in both hanging and table lamps. In the 1920s Muller Frères produced a large range of them adorned with bronze serpents, flowers, and twining leaves.

By 1925 the Art Nouveau style of lighting was superseded by much more modern lamps. Pierre Chareau made several models of his "La Religieuse" lamp in different sizes from table to floor-standing. It had a mahogany base topped with bronze and alabaster which gave it the look of a coiffed nun. He also made lamps in a similar style for hanging from the ceiling.

By 1930 lighting design moved on again when Jacques Adnet brought out wall-mounted neon strip lights and, in the same year, Perzel produced table lamps in pale blue and cream cast metal as well as an upward-lighting floor lamp that looked like a double trumpeted flower. Other modern-looking table lamps from the 1930s had glass globes shaped like doughnuts.

Today's fashionable triangular wall lights made their first appearances in the 1930s: Eckhart Muthesis produced some for the vast furnishing scheme commissioned by the Maharajah of Indore for his palace.

Lamp design became even more adventurous in the 1960s with the Valenti floor lamp by Olaf von Bohr — its shade made from spirally mounted strips of satinized steel. In 1972 Gae Aulenti designed the Artemide Pileo floor lamp, and a desk Anglepoise designed by Gaetano in 1971 was exhibited at the New York Metropolitan Museum of Modern Art. The Anglepoise lamp was originally designed in the 1930s but its structure is timeless.

Plastic is now used extensively in lighting, and one of the most unusual lamps is the Astroide plastic and metal model lamp designed by Ettore Sottssas in 1968. It is pink on one side and blue on the other.

LEFT *Turn-of-the-century cut-glass banquet lamp.*

COST	● ● ●
OUTLOOK	● ● ● ●

RIGHT *"Oiseau de Feu," a Lalique semi-circular luminaire.*

COST	● ● ● ● ●
OUTLOOK	● ● ● ● ●

Trade Catalogues

Although there are specialist collectors of trade catalogs, most are purchased by the enthusiast who actually collects the objects illustrated or is engaged in a similar trade today. They are ideal for dating collections and, of course, for revealing to the uninitiated the value of some forgotten object long ago consigned to the attic. They are also a useful source of background information. At the height of their popularity, these old trade catalogs served the function of bringing the sole visual image of a range of goods to the prospective purchaser,

and as a result they were often printed to the highest possible standard on good-quality paper. They reflect the fashion trends of the day in everything from home furnishings, toys, and clothes to some cunningly devised gadgets and more sophisticated scientific instruments.

Their value is usually dictated by the popularity of the objects they portray; those for toys, fishing tackle, tools, furniture, clothing, china, and the like are highly prized, particularly if they are from well-known firms or famous department stores. Those for such things as rainwater heads have a more limited appeal.

*Philips radio with Chinese
lacquerwork design.*

CHAPTER FIVE

Housewares

REFRIGERATORS & CLEANERS

KITCHEN EQUIPMENT

BAKELITE & PLASTICS

TELEPHONES, RADIOS, & TVs

CLOCKS

TINS

Introduction

THERE HAS BEEN a revolution on the domestic front since 1900. At the beginning of the century, the kitchen was modernized by the introduction of gas for lighting and cooking but, before very long, that innovation was overshadowed by the introduction of electricity, which was to transform domestic life.

Kitchens in the 19th century were dark and inconvenient places in which conditions had not changed for centuries. By 1930, however, it was every woman's ambition to bring her kitchen up to date and, providing she had money available, she could do it.

In the 1931 edition of Mrs Beeton's *Household Management*, the labor-saving home was glowingly described as a place where "lifts and trolleys will relieve servants of most of the carrying. Every bedroom, besides having hot and cold water laid on, will have its gas fire or electric radiator. There will be cookers, boilers and toasters, not forgetting a telephone and perhaps an electrically controlled clock. Electric suction sweepers and mechanical scrubbers will make the housemaid's job a sinecure!"

That must have sounded enough like a dream to most women — especially housemaids — at the time, and they would have found it hard to believe that in only a few more years kitchens were to be turned into mechanized workbenches humming with microwave ovens and electronic washing machines.

Collections of old kitchen equipment and fittings, like the displays in York's City Museum, make visitors realize the extent of the revolution that has taken place in the kitchen during their own lifetimes.

Ashtray, lamp, perfume bottle, and box in plastic, 1920s.

Postwar kitchen from Modern Homes Illustrated, *1947.*

"Robin Day" television, British Design Award winner of 1957, made by Pye Ltd.

Ekco Consolette radio, Model SH25, from 1931.

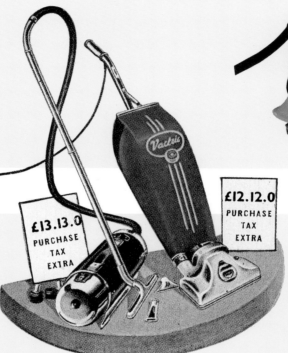

£13.13.0 PURCHASE TAX EXTRA

£12.12.0 PURCHASE TAX EXTRA

Vactric vacuum cleaners sweeping British homes in the 1940s.

New-shape electric iron, designed by Christian Barman for H.M.V. in 1937.

K.B. toaster, model FB10C, designed by Lawrence Griffin, 1950.

Food mixer by Rotel AG, an award winner in Switzerland in 1959.

Rooster napkin rings cast in Catalin plastic.

Whimsical "sleeping beaker" produced in melamine to advertise a bedtime drink.

Smart and slimline flashlight from Durabeam.

Refrigerators & Cleaners

AMONG THE MOST attractive and functionally successful designs of the 20th century were those of American refrigerators in the late 1930s. Those chunky, reassuringly solid machines with iceboxes on top have never been surpassed in kitchen design, and some are still being used by owners who dread having to replace them with more up-to-date models.

Refrigeration came into the home early in the 20th century. It was first introduced in 1880 to bring frozen mutton from New South Wales to England and, about the same time, to store meat in the Chicago warehouses. What made it available for every household, however, was the growing utilization of electricity in a domestic context. By 1902 the Sears Roebuck catalog was advertising ice cream freezers and refrigerators for "rooming houses," and from there it was only a matter of time before every household wanted one.

Electrically powered vacuum cleaners were not far behind refrigerators. The vacuum cleaner was invented by an Englishman, A. Cecil Booth, in 1901, and it was taken from house to house in a horse-drawn cab with the tube being brought in through the window for cleaning. Ladies used to give tea parties and watch this operation going on.

The first electrically powered vacuum cleaner was invented in 1908 by the American James Spangler, a member of the Hoover family, and two years later the Baby Daisy cleaner was brought out in England. It took two people to handle those early cleaners, however, and the boom did not start until a more manageable vacuum was introduced. By 1912, the BVC vacuum became popular and was rapidly followed by the Cyclone and Daisy sweepers of 1914. The Daisy was the first machine to suck dirt into a cloth bag at its back.

ABOVE *Philco 1930s refrigerator with flush door.*

| COST | ● ● | |
| OUTLOOK | ● ● | |

BELOW *Cylinder cleaner Model 25 from Electrolux, 1923.*

| COST | ● ● | |
| OUTLOOK | ● ● | |

BELOW *A classic Hoover Junior upright vacuum cleaner, 1936.*

| COST | ● ● ● | |
| OUTLOOK | ● ● ● ● | |

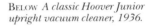

LEFT *England's first vacuum cleaner: the Baby Daisy of 1910. Two people were needed to operate this machine, and it was not until 1912, when a more manageable machine was introduced, that cleaners were bought in any number.*

COST	● ● ● ●
OUTLOOK	● ●

BELOW *An advertisement for a gas refrigerator that appeared in the 1930s.*

COST	● ● ●
OUTLOOK	● ●

BELOW *An advertisement for a vacuum cleaner from* Modern Homes Illustrated, *1947.*

COST	● ● ●
OUTLOOK	● ●

This GAS REFRIGERATOR

- is absolutely silent
- has no moving parts
- has nothing to wear out or go wrong
- can't interfere with the wireless

AND IT'S YOURS FOR ONLY — **2/6 A WEEK**

A GAS REFRIGERATOR is easily the most convenient way of keeping your food safe and appetising — of stopping the waste of those 'left-overs' — of keeping butter firm and salads crisp and milk sweet and safe — of making possible a whole lot of exciting new ices and iced dishes and cold drinks.

A GAS REFRIGERATOR is absolutely silent, cheap to run, and so reliable that it is *guaranteed* for five years. And the model illustrated is big enough for an ordinary family, yet costs only 2/6 a week. Go round to your local gas showrooms, and see what a lot of room there is in this refrigerator—but how little space it takes up!

ISSUED BY THE BRITISH COMMERCIAL GAS ASSOCIATION
Gas Industry House, 1, Grosvenor Place, London, S.W.1.

£13.13.0 PURCHASE TAX EXTRA

£12.12.0 PURCHASE TAX EXTRA

GO AND TAKE A GOOD LOOK AT THE VACTRIC

It's all-British—and it's in the shops NOW!

Judge for yourself the excellent finish, quietness and lightness — and the effortless efficiency of the double-suction motor. See how carpets are protected by the simple brush-height adjustment for varying thicknesses of pile; the patent device that lowers the handle to floor level for cleaning under low furniture.

Ask your Electrical Dealer, Electricity Supply Company or Store to demonstrate to-day.

Vactric

THE EFFORTLESS CLEANERS

THAT ARE SWEEPING

THE COUNTRY

VACTRIC LIMITED. 149, REGENT STREET, LONDON, W.1

Kitchen Equipment

THE VOGUE FOR COLLECTING Victorian kitchen equipment has been superseded in recent years by a preference for equipment from the earlier years of this century. Avid collectors often use the things they find in preference to more modern plastic gadgets.

Enameling was popular in the 1920s, and good examples of white enamel storage jars for flour, sugar, and the like can be found, preferably with the names printed on them in stark blue or black letters. Another area of interest is early examples of kitchen gadgets like egg whisks. One of the first was Holt's Patent Egg Beater, made in the U.S. in 1900, and the design has changed little over the years.

A good example of kitchen scales was the early 20th-century Acme Household Scale. Toasters and electric irons had no thermostats when they were first marketed by the General Electric Company in 1913, and housewives had to wait until 1930 before the Mysto iron, the first with a thermostat, appeared.

Collectors seek out examples of every development in the kitchen — electric coffee grinders perhaps, or the first steam- or battery-operated iron. There is a wealth of material available, from home canning machines to early electric grinders. One of the earliest electric blenders is the Kenmix "55," a stately machine standing on a cherry-red power base. These early blenders are often preferred in the modern kitchen because the cutting knives are made of metal and the flasks of thick glass which is less liable to damage, easier to clean, and always looks better than plastic.

BELOW *Copper molds from early 20th-century kitchens are lasting well, and are keenly collected not just for their looks but for practical use as well.*

| COST | ● ● |
| OUTLOOK | ● ● ● |

LEFT *An early twentieth-century iron coffee grinder.*

COST	● ●
OUTLOOK	● ● ●

LEFT *Painted tin scales of the 1920s from the United States.*

COST	● ●
OUTLOOK	● ● ●

BELOW *The Russell Hobbs Futura "Forgettle Kettle," 1973.*

COST	● ●
OUTLOOK	● ● ●

ABOVE *A flour container and bread box familiar in granny's kitchen, and much in favor today.*

COST	● ●
OUTLOOK	● ● ●

RIGHT *Westinghouse 1950 toaster, styled to look like an automobile, with sophisticated timer and thermostat controls.*

COST	● ●
OUTLOOK	● ● ●

Bakelite & Plastics

RIGHT *Bakelite flask, 1930s.*

COST	● ●
OUTLOOK	● ●

BELOW *Plastics were a favorite material of the 1920s and 1930s. A wide variety of household objects could take on all the bold and unusual shapes, brilliant colors, and marble or pearly surfaces beloved of Art Deco designers. This selection includes cigarette boxes, spectacle cases and bookends.*

COST	● ●
OUTLOOK	● ●

BAKELITE WAS THE world's first truly inexpensive material that could be used for an amazing variety of purposes. It was a synthetic resin prepared by the chemical interaction of a phenol, such as was found in coal tar, with a derivative of methyl alcohol. The discovery was made in 1909 by an American research chemist called Leo Baekeland, founder of the Nepera Chemical Company of Yonkers, N.Y.

Bakelite was originally developed for use in the ignition systems of airplane engines and as an electrical insulator but the potential of the new material was rapidly realized by manufacturers of radio cases, ashtrays, dollhouse furniture, perfume bottle holders, jewelry, vases, airplane propellers, and tableware.

Bakelite was originally amber-colored but later the most usual colors were cream or black. It could be made very cheaply but its drawback was that it cracked easily. However, it superseded the use of wood or china for many small things and led the field as a material for making inexpensive articles until the discovery of plastics in the 1960s.

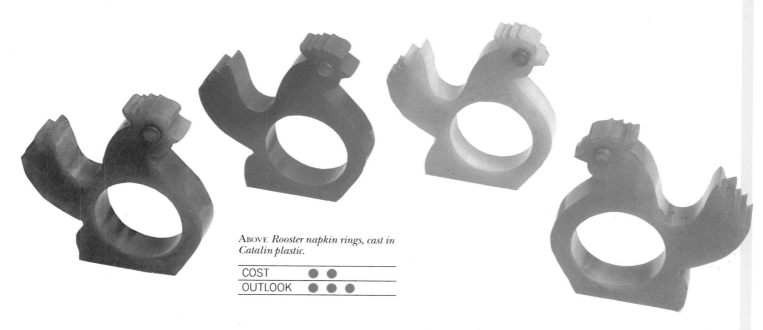

ABOVE *Rooster napkin rings, cast in Catalin plastic.*

COST	● ●
OUTLOOK	● ● ●

ABOVE *An amusingly whimsical "sleeping beaker" produced in melamine as part of an advertising campaign for a bedtime drink.*

COST	● ●
OUTLOOK	● ●

RIGHT *A highly collectible "smoker's friend" box, a dry measure scoop, and a sundae dish, all from the 1920s. Here Bakelite appears in its most familiar colors: a range of amber and brown.*

COST	● ●
OUTLOOK	● ● ●

Telephones, Radios, & TVs

LEFT *Britain's first molded telephone, designed in 1950 and introduced by the G.P.O. in 1958, its squat black shape soon to become a familiar sight.*

COST	● ●
OUTLOOK	● ● ●

THE FIRST TELEPHONES were wall mounted and worked by a crank handle. They were followed by standard models with the earpiece hanging at the side. These were in use until the late 1930s, when they were supplanted by squat, all-in-one models, usually in black.

This style of phone is now among the most desirable for collectors and home decorators, having supplanted the reproductions of French rococo brass-mounted machines that were popular in the 1970s. The black 1940s phones have a pleasantly solid appearance and are reassuringly weighty in the hand.

Broadcasting by radio is very much a development of the 20th century: Marconi only transmitted the first radio signals from shore to a ship at sea over a distance of 18 miles (25 kilometers) in December 1897.

The potential of broadcasting was quickly appreciated, particularly in the U.S., where it was developed by private enterprise. The first attempt at broadcasting music there was in 1916 by Dr. Lee De Forest. In Britain, the development was slower and it was not until 1922 that the British Broadcasting Company was transmitting on a regular basis.

The first receivers were built by enthusiasts and date from around 1919. They were "cat's whisker" sets which had to be listened to through headphones. By the end of the 1920s, however, manufacturers were turning out more up-to-date receivers every year. By the outbreak of World War II, most households owned a radio set and the broadcasting system was used for keeping up public morale and transmitting messages, both general and clandestine, to underground agents.

Prewar radio sets were often very attractive, encased as they were in wooden cabinets of attractive design with fretwork panels over the loudspeakers. Makers of some of the more appealing sets included Ambassador, Pye, and Cossor. Some of those old sets produced a mellow tone which has never been matched by present-day transmitters.

The 1930s craze for streamlining meant that some very "modern" sets were produced, decorated with mirrors, accent stripes, and white paint. A mid-1930s designer who specialized in this was Walter Dorman Teague.

The postwar period saw a wide application of bakelite and plastic to the making of radios. White bakelite was a favorite material for smaller, shelf-top models. With the passage of time radios grew less bulky and there was a vogue for portables designed like small suitcases with plastic grilles, chrome handles, and leather trim.

Later developments in transistorization meant that the sets grew smaller and could be operated by batteries. In the 1960s the first radio alarm sets appeared, and in the 1970s radio listening was revolutionized by the appearance of the first "Walkman" sets.

Though many households in America had television sets by the 1940s, few homes in Europe had them until at least ten years later. The earliest wooden sets were bulky with small, rounded screens and little to recommend them artistically. Because of their unattractiveness, some manufacturers attempted to disguise them as items of furniture and sets with sliding wooden doors that looked like cabinets were most admired.

However, as televisions slimmed down, they were fitted with brass-tipped legs and became part of the domestic décor. By the 1960s plastic took over from wood for making the cases, and today's sets come in a wide variety of colors and styles, though they are still fairly space-consuming; future developments should trim them down considerably.

BELOW *There are still radios stored away and forgotten in attics — like this Pye model "MM" of 1932. Any Art Deco styling adds to the value.*

COST	● ● ●
OUTLOOK	● ● ● ●

Typewriters

ABOVE *One of the earliest T.V. and radio sets, designed for Ekco, 1936.*

COST	● ● ●
OUTLOOK	● ● ●

BELOW *Ekco 1938 radio UAW78, designed by Misha Black.*

COST	● ● ●
OUTLOOK	● ● ●

ABOVE *Molded Phenolic 19 inch television set Type TV12A, from Bush Radio, 1949.*

COST	● ●
OUTLOOK	● ●

LEFT *Brionvega television, designed by M. Zanuso and R. Sapper, Italy, 1962.*

COST	● ●
OUTLOOK	● ● ●

Although the first typewriter, designed by the American Christopher Sholes, appeared in 1874, it was not until 1900 that its potential for transforming office life was really recognized. The introduction of typewriters was also socially significant because it meant that women had their first entrée into commerce and business. Their "gentle touch" was thought to make them better typists than the men who had previously done most clerking jobs. The earliest maker of typewriters on a large scale was Remington, but hundreds of other manufacturers soon appeared, turning out a wide variety of styles and mechanisms. Though most had a platen bar and a semicircle of letters on the ends of metal bars, the Lambart typewriter, produced by the Gramophone and Typewriter Co. of America around 1900, had a dial like a telephone. More conventional looking was the Blickensderfer of 1910 which was the first successful portable machine. Other popular makes were by Underwood and Olivers. With the exception of the Salter Standard No. 7, which had three rows of keys instead of four and a type bar swinging down from the top onto the platen, the design of typewriters, and the QWERTY arrangement of their keys, changed little from the beginning of the century. The main innovations since then have been electric typewriters in the 1950s and word processors in the 1970s.

Clocks

ONE OF THE CHARACTERISTIC clocks of the 20th century is the grandmother clock, a scaled-down long-case clock, often in a case with Art Nouveau decorations. Grandmother clocks were popular for smaller households, and today good examples bring high prices from collectors.

Many of the most distinguished jewelers of the period also produced elegant table clocks. In the 1920s Lalique and Jean Goulden made expensive clocks for discriminating customers; Goulden's 1928 silver and enamelled Art Deco clock is worth a great deal of money today. In the 1940s Cartier in Paris made clocks in gold, silver, rock crystal, and diamonds.

For the cheaper end of the market, some very attractive enameled clocks were produced in the 1920s, especially the ones with "butterfly wing" faces that shimmered and shone in a myriad of colors. The first electric clocks were often made in bakelite or, later, plastic, and tomorrow's collectibles include nursery clocks with Mickey Mouse faces and 1960s alarm clocks that play tunes.

LEFT *Art Nouveau long-case clock by Jacques Gruber — a true collector's item.*

COST	● ● ● ● ●
OUTLOOK	● ● ● ● ●

BELOW *Art Deco originality: the Planetary Desk Clock by Cartier.*

COST	● ● ● ● ●
OUTLOOK	● ● ● ● ●

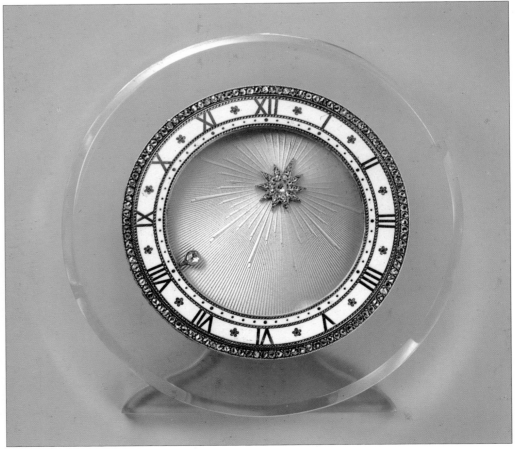

ABOVE *A calendar table clock with adjustable day and date by Cartier, Paris.*

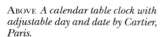

COST	● ● ● ● ●
OUTLOOK	● ● ● ● ●

RIGHT *An Ingersoll alarm clock in cream urea.*

COST	● ●
OUTLOOK	● ● ● ●

ABOVE *Art Nouveau Cymric silver clock by Liberty.*

COST	● ● ● ●
OUTLOOK	● ● ● ●

Cameras

George Eastman's invention of roll film at the end of the 19th century made miniaturization of cameras possible and opened up the industry of camera making. Now it was possible for people to buy a camera that could be easily transported from place to place.

Old and rare cameras like the 1935 Thornton Pickard F2 Ruby Speed are expensive, but less pricey makes to look out for include the German Ernemann Ermanox, Rollei, Luzo, Soho, Tenax, Deck Rullo, Contax, Robot, and Linhof.

Miniature cameras disguised as watches or cigarette lighters began to appear in the first decade of the century and included the Ticka watch-pocket-camera of George Houghton which went on sale in 1905. The most expensive of the miniaturized cameras is perhaps the Ben Akiba walking-stick-handle camera that sells for four figures.

Tins

BECAUSE THEY ARE so attractive to look at and can be found in an amazing range of shapes and sizes, decorated tins are a favorite subject for collecting.

Color printing on tin was perfected in the late 19th century and, by 1900, manufacturers were turning their ingenuity to devising unusual shapes for tins. The cookie manufacturers, Huntley & Palmer of Reading, had their tins made by a family-associated firm, Huntley, Boorne & Stevens, as well as by Barclay & Fry of London, and led the market with tins shaped like purses, trunks, pillar boxes, Toby jugs, or books. An Art Nouveau tin that went on sale in 1914 had a polished lid which could be used as a mirror, and in 1924 Huntley & Palmer's cookies were sold in tins like Egyptian urns because of the enthusiasm aroused by Howard Carter's discovery of Tutankhamen's tomb in 1923. Some unusual tins — windmills (made between 1924 and 1927) and a baby carriage with a baby inside (1930) — had moving parts and could be used as toys after the cookies were eaten.

Other cookie and cracker manufacturers also used tins as a selling gimmick. Among them were Macfarlane Lang, Jacobs, McVitie & Price, and Crawfords, who had some tins designed by Mabel Lucie Attwell.

Confectionery manufacturers — Sharps, Palm Toffees, Rowntree, Macintosh, and Fry — also realized the sales potential of attractive tins. Victory V lozenges were sold in eye-catching tins, some shaped like trains or trolley cars.

Tin collectors today specialize in makers or types. Some seek out tins painted with themes from nursery rhymes or fairy tales. Mazzawattee Tea was sold in tins painted with fairytale characters. Tins were brought out to commemorate special events like coronations, and during World War I tins containing chocolate and cigarettes were distributed to men at the Front. One of these was a gold-colored tin embossed with the head of Princess Mary sent out as a gift by the British Grocers Federation in 1914.

ABOVE *Coronation cookie tin of 1911 picturing Queen Alexandra, who was a popular favorite. This tin is from Mackenzie and Mackenzie.*

COST	● ●	
OUTLOOK	● ● ●	

BELOW *A rare W. Crawford & Sons 1920s "Meteor" Racing Car cracker tin, with scarlet and silver stripes and a hinged flap to reveal the crackers within.*

COST	● ● ●	
OUTLOOK	● ● ● ●	

ABOVE *Alice in Wonderland cottage cookie tin with the Mad Hatter's tea party in the garden, from Macfarlane and Lang, 1938.*

COST	● ●	
OUTLOOK	● ● ●	

LEFT *A highly decorative 1920s Egyptian-style tin inspired by Tutankhamun, from Dunmore and Son.*

COST	● ●
OUTLOOK	● ● ●

BELOW *Alice and the Red Queen, Tweedledum and Tweedledee, and Humpty Dumpty feature on this turn-of-the-century cracker tin made by Jacob & Co..*

COST	● ●
OUTLOOK	● ● ●

ABOVE *A 1924 British guardsman candy container of lithographed tinplate, from J. Lyons.*

COST	● ●
OUTLOOK	● ● ●

ALICE, & THE RED QUEEN.

Deco dance by Verdago, c. 1925.

CHAPTER SIX

Silver & Metalware

FIGURES

CUTLERY

HOLLOWWARE

VANITY CASES

Introduction

THE PRICE OF SILVER bullion is one of the most sensitive in international finance, and that fluctuation affects the price of most silver articles. Not long ago, elegant Queen Anne teapots were being sold for their bullion price but the market has recovered in recent years and now collectors are valuing silver items for their design and artistry.

In the early 20th century silver was a favorite metal with artists because of its color, malleability, and soft appeal. Art Nouveau jewelers in particular enjoyed working with it, turning out tableware and objects of decoration like buttons, buckles, and linked chain belts.

Silver tableware continued to be as popular as it was with the Victorians, but designs changed as the years passed, streamlined and pared-down until we arrive at the Scandinavian designs of the present day, which owe much of their inspiration to designers like Charles Rennie Mackintosh and the Dane Georg Jensen.

Sterling silver and silver plate were used to make a huge variety of both decorative and useful items. For the days of big dinner parties, silver menu-holders were produced; Omar Ramsden made some in the shape of galleons. Dining-table decorations in the shape of silver birds and animals became popular in the 1930s. The earlier ones are worth buying but copies made up to the present day in Italy and Spain are often of inferior craftsmanship. Salt and pepper sets in highly original designs were widely produced. Though electric lighting was soon in use nearly everywhere, candlesticks were still popular for decoration, and Georg Jensen's firm turned out squat and elegant sticks designed by Sigvar Bernadotte in the 1960s.

Dressing-table sets backed with silver and silver photograph frames were hugely popular. Frames in Art Nouveau styles are very sought after, but buyers should take care that they are not damaged because thin sheet silver was used to make them. Less ornate Art Deco frames in silver or pewter make very good buys.

Memories of the Jazz Age are evoked by period cocktail shakers, often in silver but more commonly in electroplate. Designers also made ice-buckets, long-handled spoons for stirring Martinis, and fluted strainers for pouring cocktails through crushed ice. Less racy items are toast racks which Christopher Dresser designed for the electroplate manufacturers Hukin & Heath.

The vast expansion in the production of electroplate was a 20th-century development. In the 1970s electroplate was dismissed by collectors, but today it is one of the most desirable collectibles because of the style and elegance achieved by some designers.

One of a pair of silver candelabra, with five cup-shaped candle nozzles, designed by Georg Jensen, 1920.

Silver-gilt novelty eggs designed by Stuart Devlin, c. 1960.

Art Nouveau liqueur set by Patriz Huber, c. 1900.

Cymric silver candlesticks showing strong Celtic shape; by Archibald Knox for Liberty's, London, 1902.

Figures of Pierrot and Pierrette by Demêtre Chiparus.

Covered bowl of silver and rose quartz, c. 1928, by Jean E. Puiforcat.

Stainless steel tableware by Georg Jensen Silversmiths, Copenhagen, 1946.

Silver-plated coffee service by Sabattini showing the influence of Expressionism in the 1950s.

Cigarette packet holders made in leathers such as morocco, hide, pigskin, and calf.

"Chinese Black": cutlery designed by David Mellor and made in Sheffield, 1975.

Silver duck spoons and saltcellars designed by Sarah Jones, London, 1983.

Silver-copper bowl by Michael Rowe, 1980.

Figures

DURING THE ART NOUVEAU period many artists saw the artistic possibilities of casting bronze in flowing shapes and, as one of the themes that inspired them was the idealization of the female form, they made a large number of statues of women, draped and undraped. These figures are in the top bracket of present-day collectibles.

At the turn of the century dilettantes worshipped actresses and dancers like Sarah Bernhardt, Loie Fuller, and Cleo de Merode and sculptors produced figures of them, particularly Fuller, a dancer who specialized in draping scarves around herself. Pierre Fix-Masseau, Luis Chalon, Agathon Leonard, and Paul Roche all made statues in fluid poses, starting a vogue, and were imitated by others who turned out bronze or alloy statuettes, often with ivory hands and faces, mounted on bases of onyx or marble.

The chief centers for producing bronze and ivory figures were Paris and Vienna. Some very beautiful works were made like Becquerel's 1920s figure of a woman leading a greyhound and wearing a patterned cloak. The idea of the woman as huntress was taken up by Lorenzl in the 1930s with his figure of a naked woman running after two leashed dogs. This figure was much copied by lesser artists.

The aim of many artists was to interpret movement, and series of figures of dancers were popular, especially those by Claire Jeanne Colinet, one of the few women to work in this field.

The Rumanian Demêtre Chiparus made figures of pierrots and columbines and K. Lorenzl represented the "new woman" wearing fashionable pajama suits.

Because the most expensive figures were produced for rich collectors, some artists, especially Charol and Bruno Zach, specialized in erotic figures. Zach's sado-masochistic women posture in black leather, carry whips, and seem to have stepped straight out of Christopher Isherwood's Berlin novel *Mr. Norris Changes Trains.*

By the 1930s another German artist, F. Preiss (his first name is not known), was turning out figures exalting Nazi ideals of Aryan supremacy. Figures very similar to his were also produced by Prof. Otto Poerzl, who may have been Preiss himself using a pseudonym.

At the same time British artists were specializing in metal figure production, although there was no significant school of Art Nouveau sculpture in Britain. Makers of bronzes were influenced by teachers like Aime-Jules Dalou, who taught at Kensington and Lambeth art schools from 1880.

Charles Sykes created his "Spirit of Ecstasy" as a car figurehead for Rolls-Royce in 1911 and his work later influenced silversmith Phoebe Stabler. There were also sculptors of

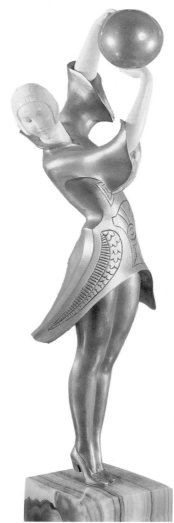

ABOVE *Girl holding a silver ball, a sculpture in bronze and ivory signed L.I.P., the pose of the figure showing movement arrested in metal.*

COST	● ● ● ●
OUTLOOK	● ● ● ●

OPPOSITE RIGHT *Snake Dancer by Demêtre Chiparus — exotic and mysterious.*

COST	● ● ● ● ●
OUTLOOK	● ● ● ● ●

BELOW *Whenever the name of Demêtre Chiparus appears, as on these Pierrot and Pierrette figures, made in France in the early 20th century, there is an exotic style and movement to the sculptures, and prices are high.*

COST	● ● ● ● ●
OUTLOOK	● ● ● ●

Trophies

imposing bronze statues including Sir Alfred Gilbert, creator of "Eros" in Piccadilly Circus and the memorial to Queen Alexandra in Marlborough Gate.

In 1911 George Frampton produced the statue of Peter Pan in London's Kensington Gardens. Auguste Rodin and Jacob Epstein also worked in London, Epstein arriving there in 1905. Rodin's work, with its unfinished, raw, energy-charged look, started a new school of sculpture which continues to influence artists.

The style of trophies and cups awarded in races, golf tournaments, and similar contests has changed little throughout the century. Racing trophies in particular, which are often made of solid silver, have tended to retain a florid Victorian style with a good deal of decoration. When they come up for sale, unless they were awarded for a very special race or to a famous horse or a famous owner, they usually sell for their bullion price. A silver gilt cup was presented to Lily Langtry when a horse she owned won a race, and the owner's name engraved on the cup made a vast difference in its price.

Models of horses and jockeys are more desirable racing trophies from a collector's point of view. They are often sculpted by famous artists such as Phoebe Stabler or P. Bonheur, who made some beautiful figures of racehorses. In the golfing world, trophies in the shape of golfers, if well made, can be expensive.

Cutlery

THE MAN MOST RESPONSIBLE for the look of modern cutlery is Georg Jensen, who made tableware until World War II and whose company continues to produce some of the most elegant cutlery today. In the early years of the century Jensen's silver, though pared down compared to the heavy pieces of the previous century, was embellished with distinctive Art Nouveau touches like clusters of flowers and fruit, particularly pineapples. Later, however, these decorations became progressively more simplified until we arrive at the stark simplicity of today's Scandinavian tableware.

Many distinguished artists worked for the Jensen company including Johan Rohde who made pieces with solid handles and curved decorative finials in silver-colored metal. In the 1920s Harald Nielsen made Pyramide table silver with large circular bowls on the spoons.

Among independent silversmiths some elegant cutlery was produced: Jean E. Puirforcat made dessert knives with a plain elongated line; Peter Behrens designed square-bowled spoons; and C.J. Begeer made silver teaspoons with oval bowls and flower finials.

When Elkington & Co. of Sheffield discovered how to make nickel-plated silver in the 1870s, it became possible for a far larger section of society to buy well-designed cutlery, and a set of silver (or plate) became a most popular wedding present. Relics of past weddings can be found at every auction sale in the silk-lined boxes of fish knives and forks or fruit knives, rarely used by their owners. Fruit knives with mother-of-pearl handles are the most desirable.

Silver was also given as a present to newborn babies — usually spoons with "pushers," napkin rings, or christening mugs. These, too, were rarely used, and when they turn up for sale their value is linked to the current price of bullion silver but, if they are of exceptional design or simply very pretty, the price will be pushed up.

ABOVE *"Blue Shark" cutlery designed by Svend Siune and made by Georg Jensen of Denmark.*

| COST | ● ● ● ● |
| OUTLOOK | ● ● ● |

OPPOSITE LEFT *Silver cutlery designed by C.R. Ashbee and made by the Guild of Handicraft Ltd., 1900-2.*

| COST | ● ● ● ● |
| OUTLOOK | ● ● ● |

RIGHT *Silver cutlery service by Jean Puiforcat of France.*

| COST | ● ● ● ● |
| OUTLOOK | ● ● ● ● |

Hollowware

COFFEE AND TEA SERVICES in silver, electroplate, pewter, or brass enjoyed tremendous sales from the beginning of the century. They were very popular wedding presents; to own a metal tea service was regarded as a sign of social prestige, even if it was never brought out of the glass-fronted cabinet.

The Brussels-based firm of Wolfers made tea-sets in silver with ivory knobs and handles; Christopher Dresser produced Art Nouveau styles decorated with panels of enameling or inset turquoise; other talented artists who produced hollowware were Georg Jensen, Omar Ramsden, Alwyn Carr, A.E. Jones, and Charles Ashbee.

The London store Liberty & Co. commissioned artists like Dresser, Jessie M. King, and Archibald Knox to design for their Cymric range of silverware which was launched in 1899. Designs were based on the curvilinear scrolls in the Book of

Kells. Because of the enthusiasm with which they were greeted, a cheaper range was made in pewter, called the Tudric range.

As the century progressed the shape of tea and coffee pots moved with fashion, gradually becoming simpler and more streamlined with less decoration and engraving. In the 1930s coffee sets slanting like speeding arrows were popular, as were the Modernist styles of French and Italian silversmiths.

The progress of design can be charted through Sabbatini's Christophle jug of the 1950s, with its flared body, small spout and open loop handle, to the trendsetting modern design for a silver and rosewood coffee set made by Paul Belvoir in 1986. Tall, spare, and elegant, it had strips of rosewood separating the handles from the bodies of the jugs. The rosewood provided not only decoration, but acted as an insulator as well.

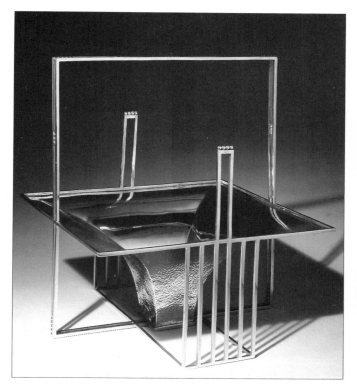

ABOVE *Silver fruit basket of avant garde design by Josef Hoffman, 1904.*

COST	● ● ● ●
OUTLOOK	● ● ●

BELOW *Coffee service, designed by Stuart Devlin when still a student at the Royal College of Art, made by Wakely and Wheeler, London, 1959.*

COST	● ● ●
OUTLOOK	● ●

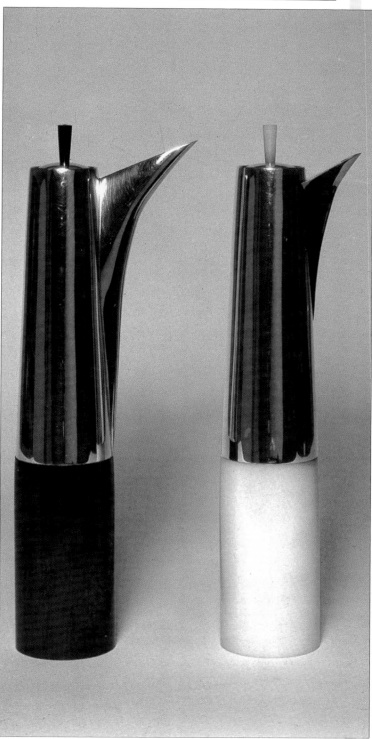

OPPOSITE LEFT *Five-piece tea and coffee service in silver and ivory by Charles Boyton.*

COST	● ● ● ●
OUTLOOK	● ●

BELOW *Silver-plated cocktail set in distinctive Art Deco style from the Paris workshops of Donald Desney, c. 1925.*

COST	● ● ● ●
OUTLOOK	● ● ● ●

Vanity Cases

THE WORD "VANITY" is not entirely flattering, and the image of a lady with a vanity case is one in which she is engrossed in self admiration, peering at herself in a little hand glass while repairing her make-up. The vanity case was a peculiar 20th-century piece of feminine equipment, carried in the purse and wielded like a weapon in the war between the sexes, especially in the movies.

Vanity cases, nevertheless, were popular and could be found in most purses until the late 1950s. Today they mostly turn up in yard sales or charity shops but look out for them because many were very attractive and some are quite valuable.

Vanity cases were made in precious or base metal. Some were decorated with diamonds and others with painted stencils of dogs, flowers, or crinoline ladies. Some bore the owner's initials in embossed letters but the prettiest ones were made in the 1930s and were enameled in glorious colors.

Inside the lid there was a mirror and if you buy a vanity case today, make sure the mirror isn't cracked. In the shallow body of the case there was pressed powder and a little powder puff. The more luxurious vanity cases had a sheath attached to the side for a lipstick and the Rolls Royce models also had an extra compartment for cigarettes. After years in the doldrums they are becoming popular again with collectors because they are redolent of a past era when women of the world made up their faces in public and unashamedly smoked cigarettes.

Cigarette cases

Some indication of the widespread popularity of the smoking habit can be seen in the abundance of delightful cigarette cases on the market today. They are a popular subject for collectors, mainly because they are plentiful, attractive and, although they were designed to hold only the smaller cigarettes, in use they re-create the elegance of times past.

Cigarette cases were made from gold, silver, tortoiseshell, papier mâché, and enamel. Often the decoration is concentrated on the lid, and the variety of ornament used is infinite: there may be inset precious stones, engraving, painting, or inlays of contrasting materials. The earliest examples are of formal design, demonstrating the skills of the silversmith and engraver, but once it became fashionable for women to smoke, the designs take on the bold and colorful patterns of the modernist era. Those with enamel decoration are particularly pleasing, ranging from European plated examples with pictures of animals, which sell for about $250, to stylish examples by F. Zwichl, featuring racing cars from the 1920s.

BELOW *Vanity case by Asprey from the 1920s.*

COST	● ● ●
OUTLOOK	● ● ● ●

OPPOSITE *Make-up compact with character, made of enamel and silver by Lacloche Frères c. 1920.*

COST	● ● ● ●
OUTLOOK	● ● ● ●

ABOVE *Very collectible 1920s powder compacts in metal.*

COST	● ● ●
OUTLOOK	● ● ● ● ●

BELOW *Vanity case by Asprey from the 1920s.*

COST	● ● ●
OUTLOOK	● ● ● ●

Cigarette lighters

Most of the old cigarette lighters on the market today date from around 1900, and there are still many interesting and unusual examples available at modest prices. This is a good area for investment, particularly the early experimental types and patented examples which demonstrate great ingenuity in combining different functions to good effect. There is a combined battery-operated flashlight and gas lighter, an evening purse cum dance-card lighter, and a lighter disguised to conceal a a cosmetic compact. Some of the most interesting lighters date from the period of the World War I, when they were handmade from bullet cases and other odds and ends of battle.

Simple lighters like the Osmond or Zetron, made in the Dunhill style, can be bought for less than $20, but the genuine gold Dunhill lighter, which also incorporates a watch, could cost over $1700.

Silver and enamel brooch by C.R. Ashbee, 1907.

CHAPTER SEVEN

Jewelry

NECKLACES & PENDANTS

BROOCHES

BRACELETS & EARRINGS

HAIR & DRESS ORNAMENTS

PLASTIC JEWELRY

Introduction

THE MUCH PUBLICIZED AUCTION of the Duchess of Windsor's jewelry in a huge tent on the banks of Lake Geneva in 1987 was more than just a highly successful commercial exercise by Sotheby's auction house. That sale marked a revival of interest in jewelry, and in the months after the sale, jewelry went on to be one of the most highly performing areas in the saleroom. Even during the Stock Market crash of late 1987 jewelry never faltered and investors all over the world became even more eager to put their money into precious stones.

However, during the previous decade there had been a lull in jewelry and pieces picked up then for reasonable prices subsequently showed a huge return on the investment.

In fact jewelry has always been a cyclical market, reacting early to changes of mood, and for that reason investors, as opposed to people who buy fun pieces to wear, should always seek out pieces of quality by "name" designers. Fortunately there are plenty of these to be found because the making of jewelry has always attracted fine artists.

Jewelry in the 20th century falls into three main areas — Art Nouveau, Art Deco, and Modern. These divisions are of course very fluid with Art Nouveau lingering into the Art Deco period, and both of them showing their traces even later among modern jewelry makers.

Art Nouveau jewelry made its first appearance before the turn of the century and continued until about 1914, although René Lalique, the master of them all, did not die until 1945. World War I was the watershed, however, because many of the talented craftsmen and designers, as well as their patrons, were killed. Lalique himself made no more jewelry after that war.

Art Deco jewelry was typical of the Jazz Age, a frantic period of ostentation and worship of style by people who counted themselves lucky to be alive. Their jewelry was innovative and flashy, executed in a geometric style. It is very fashionable today because it chimes in well with the spirit of our age. Art Deco was brought to a dramatic halt; the Great Depression of the 1930s was its death knell.

Later jewelry had an entirely different mood. "Jokey" in the 1940s and 1950s, it became more serious as designers searched for new methods and new materials with which to express themselves. The discoveries of the new age — plastics and acrylics, nylon, and titanium — are used today in jewelry making, and designers are bringing space-age ideas into their pieces.

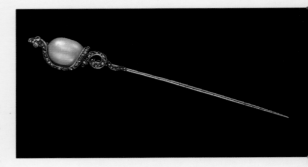

Tiepin of gold, diamond, and pearl marked Fabergé St. Petersburg; c. 1900.

Ruby, sapphire, emerald, citrine, and diamond flamingo clip for the Duchess of Windsor.

Brooch and earrings set with emeralds, c. 1950.

Enameled silver pendants with
amethysts (left) and fire opals (right);
early 20th century.

Pendant brooch of diamond,
tourmaline, and plique-à-jour by
René Lalique; early 20th century.

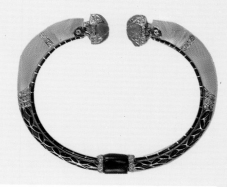

Art Deco bangle designed as two
fluted rock crystal dolphins
by Lacloche Frères c. 1920.

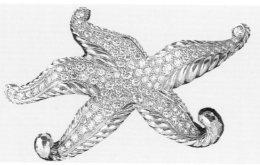

Gold and diamond starfish brooch
by Cartier, 1920s.

Peacock paste brooch from the 1930s.

Clips of sapphires and diamonds by
Boucheron c. 1940.

Brooch of diamonds and citrine from
the 1940s.

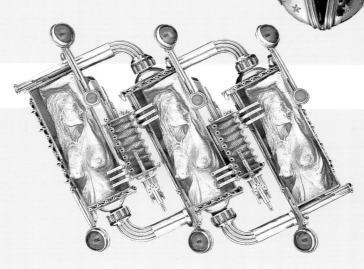

Narrative belt buckle, "Goneril,
Regan, Cordelia," in sterling silver,
by Richard Mawdsley, 1976.

Earrings and brooch of oxidized
silver and 24-carat gold by Daphne
Krinos.

Necklaces & Pendants

ABOVE *Ivory rose necklace and ivory child pendant of the 1920s.*

COST	● ● ●
OUTLOOK	● ● ● ●

THERE IS A ROMANTIC and superstitious quality about a necklace that dates back through the centuries to the days when they were thought to protect the wearer. Sometimes they were worn under the clothes for devotional reasons or to ward off witchcraft. In less developed societies today small children wander around with nothing on but a necklace from which hangs an amulet.

More ornamental necklaces can be made of gold or silver, enameled or set with gemstones, made up from ropes of pearls, amber, or garnets. They come in various lengths from the dog collar necklace — worn tight around the neck and made fashionable by Queen Alexandra at the beginning of the 20th century — to the long ropes of swinging beads (often of jade or amber) that characterized the 1920s flapper. Later still women followed the fashion of wearing black velvet ribbons around their necks with pendants or lockets attached to them.

The pearl necklace has managed to hold its place in the affections of the fashionable for most of the 20th century. Both real and artificial pearl necklaces can be found in long strings, double or triple strands, sometimes with attractive Art Deco clasps that seem too pretty to be concealed at the back of the wearer's neck — though the bobbed haircut ensured that it was displayed in the 1920s and 1930s.

Beyond the pocket of most people, the diamond necklaces produced by master jewelers of the 1930s are unbeatable for their severity of style. Cartier and Van Cleef and Arpels are names that set the collectors bidding in the big auction houses.

Modern designers are also producing eye-catching necklaces in unusual materials, some of them shaped like heavy torques and molded to curve along the collar bone in a single piece. Primitive jewelry is also popular, particularly Indian necklaces with heavy amber-type beads intermingled with smaller metal or glass ones, often with metal bells hanging from the front. Ivory — or artificial ivory — is also a favored material made up in heavy chunks strung together with ropes of finer beads.

BELOW *Art Nouveau-style peacock pendant by C.R. Ashbee, c. 1900.*

COST	● ● ●
OUTLOOK	● ● ● ●

Tutankhamen

In 1923 the discovery of Tutankhamen's tomb had a pronounced effect on jewelry design when pictures were flashed across the world of the exotic lapis lazuli jewelry found in the Pharaoh's treasure. These pieces were copied extensively and provided the inspiration for many other designs, including a gold, diamond, and sapphire Tutankhamen bracelet made by the French designers Lacloche Frères. It had patterns of Egyptian cryptographs in the colored stones set in its diamond-encrusted surface.

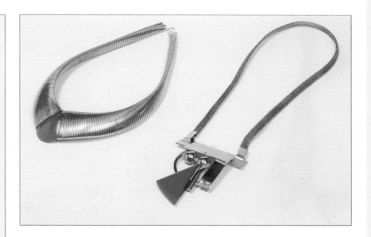

ABOVE *Deco-style jewelry in chrome and plastic.*

COST	● ●
OUTLOOK	● ●

BELOW *Necklace of flower petals preserved in a jewelry design of the 1960s by Gijs Bakker of Holland.*

COST	● ●
OUTLOOK	● ●

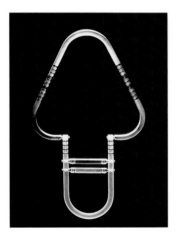

ABOVE *Acrylic and silver necklace in a clear-cut, modern style, made by David Watkins in 1975.*

COST	● ●
OUTLOOK	● ●

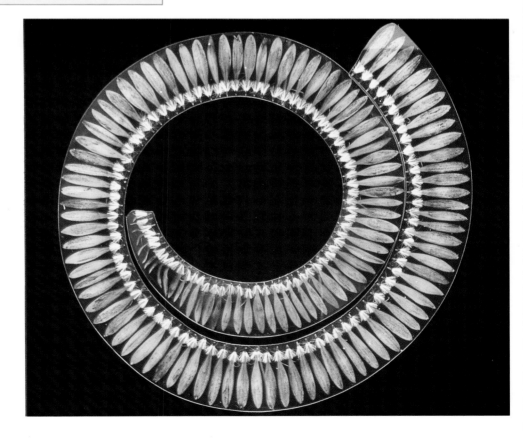

Brooches

ABOVE *A gold and plique-à-jour enamel brooch set with blue stones on the peacock plumes, made by Gautrait in the 1900s and embodying all the elements of French Art Nouveau creation and turn-of-the-century sophistication.*

| COST | ● ● ● |
| OUTLOOK | ● ● ● |

ABOVE *A fibula by Anne Marie Shillitoe in anodized titanium inlaid with tantalum and niobium, c. 1980.*

| COST | ● ● |
| OUTLOOK | ● ● ● |

ONE OF THE MOST ancient types of jewelry is the brooch. Basically it is an ornamental clasp fastened to the owner's clothing by a pin. There are examples going back to Bronze Age times when they were worn by both men and women. More recently, however, they were favored by women alone.

Designers have let their fancies free with brooches which can be found in shapes of almost every possible decorative theme. The Victorians were particularly fond of brooches but their taste ran to the heavy and florid. Brooches set with pieces of marble, with heavy cameos and even with human hair as mourning pieces were greatly prized, but in more recent times there was a reaction against such weighty objects and turn-of-the-century Art Nouveau brooches were much lighter and more delicate-looking. Art Nouveau designers also rebelled against putting valuable stones like diamonds and emeralds in brooches and produced attractive designs using horn, wood, semi-precious stones, and enameling. They were particularly fond of using filigree metal, gold, or silver to hold the decorative pieces together.

With the coming of the Art Deco period, brooches took on a more solid aspect, growing sparsely geometrical in shape and becoming once again a means of displaying the wearer's wealth. Diamond and ruby brooches or clips sparkled on

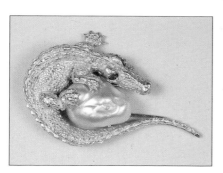

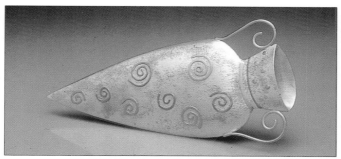

Insignia

The outbreak of World War II was marked by a new fashion for women wearing brooches with the insignia of various army regiments, the Royal Air Force, and the Royal Navy. To cater for all pockets, they were on sale set with diamonds or with paste, and both are now being collected.

women's breasts and shoulders, often in the fantastic animal or bird shapes admired and made fashionable by the late Duchess of Windsor.

This rich ostentation gradually dwindled in the different social climate of the 1940s and 1950s and it was then that jokey "costume-style" jewelry made its mark. Designers produced cartoon type animal brooches — smiling lions, donkeys with flower-filled panniers on their backs, monkeys swinging from tree branches. They were fond of using diamante, but the more expensive pieces came in solid gold with diamond or ruby eyes. Many of these valuable pieces were copied in less expensive materials and were sold in jewelry chain stores such as Ciro. In the postwar years, jewelry became more of a studied fashion accessory and was designed by prominent couturiers like Chanel or Christian Dior to complement their clothes.

Bracelets & Earrings

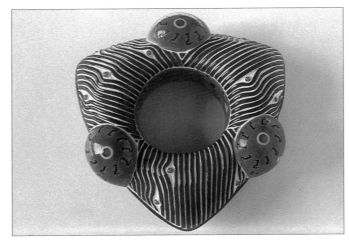

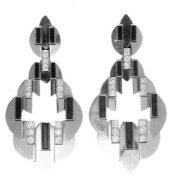

COST	● ●	
OUTLOOK	● ● ●	

ABOVE CENTER *Dramatic and highly decorative bangle with fashion impact, designed by Peter Chang.*

COST	● ●	
OUTLOOK	● ●	

A BRACELET IS A flexible band or series of links worn around the wrist; a bangle is also worn around the wrist but it is rigid. Both of these items of jewelry have been greatly favored pieces of personal adornment for men and women since primitive times. The Vikings were particularly fond of displaying their golden bracelets and one of their leaders demonstrated his power over his men by hanging his bracelets on a tree and forbidding any of his band of marauders to touch them. Today in the West the bracelet is mainly worn by women. Some men wear identity bracelets and some wear a bangle but it is in the East that the bangle is commonly worn by men, particularly Sikhs for whom it is one of the symbols of their religion.

The changing face of fashion has affected the bracelet as much as other types of jewelry. Heavy Edwardian bracelets, often made of pearls and worn on both wrists, gave way to lighter Art Nouveau creations which tuned in with the delicacy of the brooches and necklaces. In the 1920s girls wore solid slave bangles, often in gold, around their upper arms. This eye-catching fashion was superseded by more conventional bracelets, particularly by the snake or animal-headed bracelets of the 1930s and then by the heavy gold or silver charm bracelets or gold link bracelets popular in the 1940s and 1950s. Both these types of bracelet have recently been making a comeback.

Pretty bracelets and bangles, which can be bought for small sums of money, include those made in plastic in the 1940s and 1950s. There were also bangles from the same period which were manufactured to look like ivory or mottled jade. The 1950s was also the time when heavy metal arm clasps which looked like the ones worn by Roman centurions of long ago became all the rage.

For many years it has been the custom to give a christening

ABOVE *Smart and stylish 1960s earrings in gold, diamond, and enamel by Cartier.*

COST	● ● ●	
OUTLOOK	● ● ● ●	

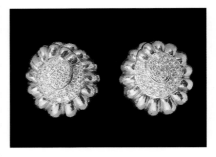

ABOVE *Distinctively American gold and diamond earrings by David Webb, 1960.*

COST	● ●	
OUTLOOK	● ● ●	

BELOW *Chromed metal "slave" bangle of the 1920s.*

| COST | ● ● |
| OUTLOOK | ● ● |

ABOVE *Silver and turquoise snake bangle with ruby eyes from the 1920s.*

| COST | ● ● |
| OUTLOOK | ● ● |

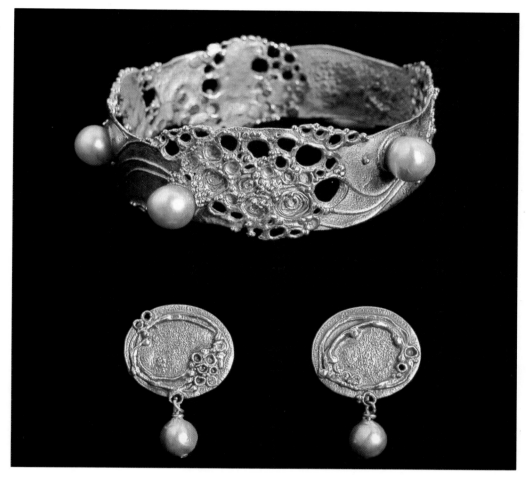

ABOVE *Silver and pearl bangle, and earrings intricately constructed of silver with oxides and 18-carat gold, incorporating brilliant-cut diamonds and hanging pearls, from the outstanding jewelry designer Gerda Flockinger, 1973-5.*

| COST | ● ● ● |
| OUTLOOK | ● ● ● ● ● |

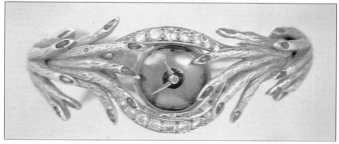

LEFT *Bracelet watch by Salvador Dali, 1960.*

| COST | ● ● ● ● ● |
| OUTLOOK | ● ● ● |

gift of a bangle or bracelet to a baby girl. The bangles are usually made of silver and engraved with flower designs, and the bracelets are often made from coral pieces or beads. Traditionally coral was given to children to protect them from evil. Earrings, ear clips, ear drops, ear loops, ear screws and ear studs are all varieties of adornment for the human ear, both male and female. They can be made in gold, silver, copper, iron, plastic, ivory, brass, platinum, or silver gilt and decorated in many ways. Habitual wearers of earrings feel undressed without them.

Hair & Dress Ornaments

BUCKLES HAVE PRESENTED an interesting fashion feature throughout the centuries. Essentially items of jewelry, they have been styled for daywear and made to sparkle for the evening. They were worn at the belt, on a garter at the knee, and on shoes. It is reported that men wore buckles as an indication of their social status, and some were so large they almost covered the whole instep.

Buckles were often included in a parure — a set of matching jewelry — and reflect changing styles. Examples include those made of precious metals and set with gemstones, and the rather ornate Victorian style of gilt, silver filigree, beads, or jet. Art Nouveau designers emphasized the use of metal, and it is buckles from this period that have become most popular with collectors today. Look for those by Theodor Fahrner, Eugene Grasset, William Comyns, Jean Despres, and Liberty & Co.

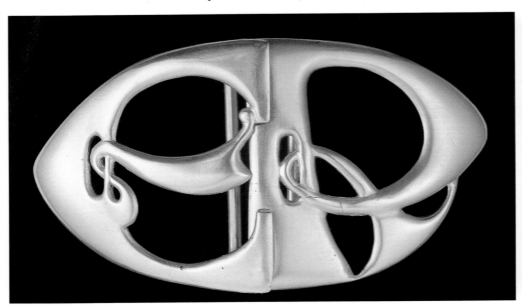

ABOVE *Silver buckle by Alexander Knox who brought Art Nouveau style to metal for Liberty & Co., London c. 1900.*

| COST | ● ● |
| OUTLOOK | ● ● ● ● |

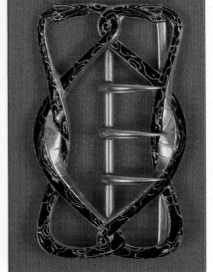

ABOVE *Belt buckle that shows the outstanding and highly sought qualities of René Lalique, c. 1900.*

| COST | ● ● ● |
| OUTLOOK | ● ● ● ● ● |

Stage shows in the 19th century had an enormous influence on fads and fashions of the period in much the same way as films and television do today. A prime example in Victorian times was Bizet's opera *Carmen,* which opened in 1875 and prompted the popularity of large tortoiseshell combs worn in the Spanish style. They continued in fashion, although often of much smaller design, until the end of the century when the hair comb again received a boost in popularity as a result of the new designs created by the Art Nouveau movement.

Although most of those found today are plain tortoiseshell examples costing a few dollars, occasionally they can be seen

110

decorated with gold and silver, or even semi-precious stones. These will obviously cost a lot more, depending on the design, with exceptional examples by established artists, such as Henri Vever or René Lalique, costing many thousands.

In the 19th century a gentleman of property adorned himself with a tiepin, dress studs, a watch chain across his chest, a collar pin, and cuff links. Today such displays would be regarded as ostentatious. Only the modest cuff links are still regarded as suitable for the conventionally well-dressed man.

Cuff links come in many materials from gold to tinplate and also in numerous designs — from college or regimental crests to those carved with the owner's initials. Many cuff links were designed with great artistry, particularly in the 1930s. At that time enameling was fashionable but some were set with gemstones, and it was also common to give engraved cuff links as presents.

There are several different styles. The most common is where a loose chain joins the decorative head of the cuff link to its back plate. Others are attached to a swivel band while some can be pressed together like a snap fastener. Cuff links are generally made in identical pairs, though unusual examples have different but complementary designs.

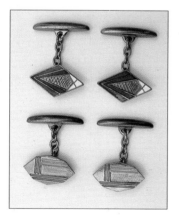

ABOVE *Enameled and gilded metal cuff links of the 1930s.*

COST	● ●
OUTLOOK	● ● ● ●

ABOVE *Gold and malachite Edwardian cuff links.*

COST	● ●
OUTLOOK	● ● ● ●

Plastic Jewelry

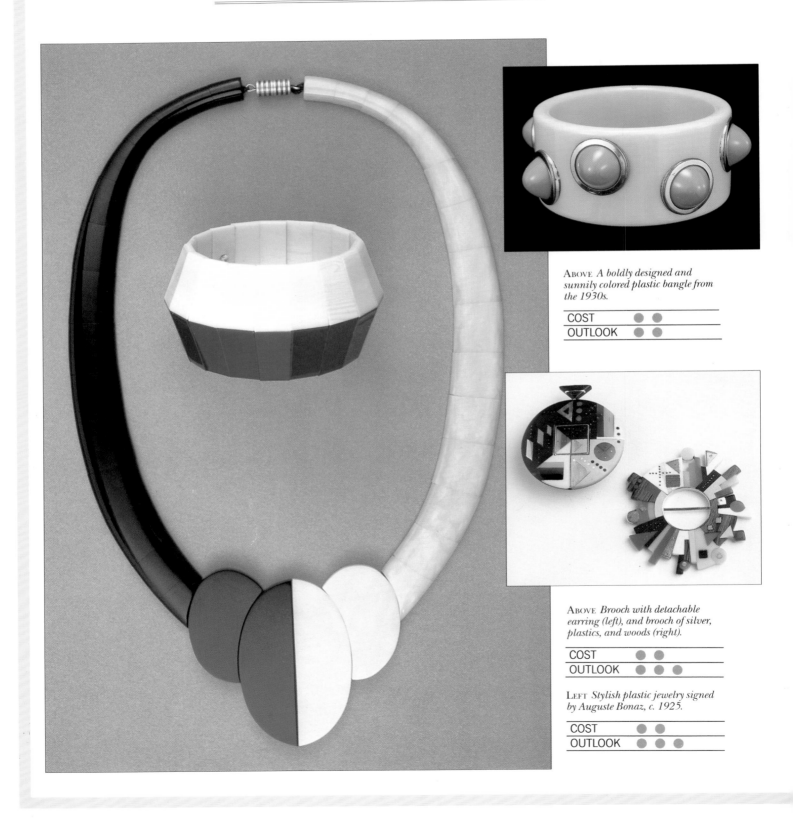

ABOVE *A boldly designed and sunnily colored plastic bangle from the 1930s.*

COST	● ●	
OUTLOOK	● ●	

ABOVE *Brooch with detachable earring (left), and brooch of silver, plastics, and woods (right).*

COST	● ●	
OUTLOOK	● ● ●	

LEFT *Stylish plastic jewelry signed by Auguste Bonaz, c. 1925.*

COST	● ●	
OUTLOOK	● ● ●	

TRADITIONALLY PLASTIC IS FUN and jokey and the cheap and cheerful aspects come to the fore best in jewelry where designers can let themselves go and not take themselves too seriously.

The commonest ingredients of plastic are celluloid and resin which make it malleable, but early plastics were brittle and difficult to mold, so it is only since the 1930s that developments in products have made it sufficiently durable and pliable to lend itself to unusual and interesting designs.

Both costume and junk jewelry is made out of plastic because it can be dyed different colors, given a metallic appearance or treated with electroplating. Vinyl or acrylic plastic are sometimes used to imitate gemstones and it can be used as the basis for artificial pearls, or to imitate amber, coral, ivory, and tortoiseshell. At times these imitations can be so good that jewelry buyers should be on their guard against fakes. It is usually possible to tell the real thing from plastic because of plastic's luster, softness, and the presence of internal bubbles in the material. If in doubt, stick a pin through it!

Since the 1970s there has been a great interest in the making of acrylic jewelry and many talented young designers are now working with it. Some of the best include David Watkins, Claus Bury, and Susanna Heron. There is nothing cheap about their work because they often combine the acrylic with gold or platinum and these pieces are the collectibles of the future.

At the cheaper end of the market, however, there has been a vogue for buying 1930s posy brooches made of plastic, or colorful lapel badges, sometimes representing Disney characters. Also popular are heavy 1950s bracelets that look as if they are made of metal and inset with gemstones but are actually made from plastic. These used to be picked up in rummage sales or in boxes of oddments; today they are more likely to be found at elevated prices in specialist stores at the smart end of town.

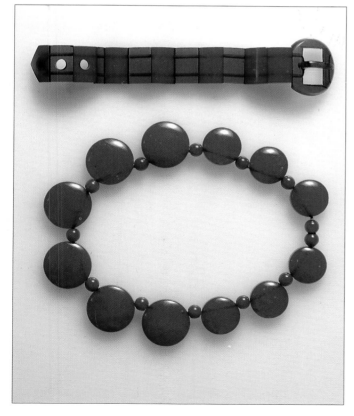

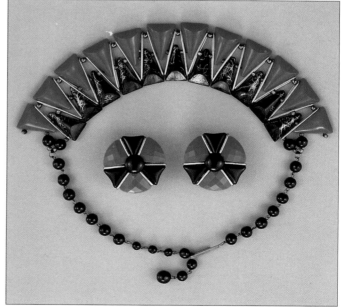

LEFT *Bakelite bracelet and plastic necklace from the 1940s-50s.*

COST	● ●
OUTLOOK	● ● ●

ABOVE *The geometric design and color contrast of these earrings and necklace suits plastic well.*

COST	● ●
OUTLOOK	● ● ●

*"Le Départ pour le Casino": mantle
designed by Worth, drawn by
Barbier, from the* Gazette du Bon
Ton, *1925.*

CHAPTER EIGHT

Fashion

COSTUME ILLUSTRATION

DAY WEAR

EVENING WEAR

SUITS & COATS

SWIMWEAR & LINGERIE

WATCHES

ACCESSORIES

Introduction

COSTUME CAN REFLECT social trends more accurately than any other aspect of the collecting world. The changing status and aspirations of women can be most fully appreciated when a tightly laced Victorian gown is compared with a typical flapper's dress of the 1920s.

The liberation of women really began during World War I when, because of a shortage of labor, women were allowed to do jobs that had always been thought of as only suitable for men. Their clothes had to be less formal and constricting, less "ladylike," to allow them to do men's work, and this trend continued over the next two decades after the exigencies of war had passed. By the time of World War II, the fashions of the time — rolled cotton headscarves and skimpy skirts — represented a utilitarian and practical attitude to women's everyday clothes. It is difficult to appreciate that this revolution took place over the lifespan of only one generation of women.

Details of fashion have changed over the years but the idea that clothes could be a means of self-expression for women has gained in importance in the 20th century.

The collecting of costume has tended to concentrate on women's clothes because it was usually women who kept their clothes. The men's clothes that have survived from the past tend either to be dress suits or ceremonial uniforms, and, if anyone is lucky enough to find a trunk of ordinary men's clothing from before World War I, they have found a treasure trove.

Beaded evening coat with batwing sleeves and hip buttoning by French designer Paul Poiret, c. 1924.

Black velvet hat with grosgrain trim, an elegant style made popular in the 1950s by models.

Op-Art quilted silk coat by leading 1960s designer Ossie Clarke modeled by Chrissie Shrimpton.

Crêpe de Rome dress designed by Brandt (left); Fausta crêpe dress designed by Bernard (right).

Spectacles given the designer treatment.

Georges Le Pape evening coat drawn by Bianchini.

Kid shoes with Art Deco asymmetric design by Pinet, 1930s.

Christian Dior's New Look that was such a joy to wear after wartime austerity.

Purse and jewelry box combined by Hermès, 1950s.

Small women grew taller on the platform soles and high heels of the 1960s.

Lipstick blouse from the 1960s by innovative designer Zandra Rhodes, popular for her flattering clothes.

Extravert sunglasses take a shaded view.

Denim jacket sewn with badges of the type much worn in the 1980s.

Costume Illustration

MEMORABILIA ASSOCIATED with entertainment is especially evocative, as all theatergoers discover when they come across old theater programs hidden away in a drawer.

Theatrical costumes have a potent magic still. Some of them can be seen displayed at the Theatre Museum in Covent Garden, London — the costume worn by Alicia Markova as Giselle, the ballet shoes signed by Margot Fonteyn, the very large costume worn by Chaliapin in *Boris Godunov* in Paris in 1908. Superb costume designs by Leon Bakst for the Diaghilev ballet appear at auction and bring prices in the $16-35,000 range.

Outstanding theatrical designers such as Bakst influenced fashion in their era, and some, like Erté, designed for the theater and for *haute couture*. Erté's distinctive art deco illustrations appeared in the fashion magazines *Vogue* and *Harper's Bazaar*. Between 1915 and 1936 he contributed 2500 drawings to *Harper's Bazaar*; 240 of them were covers, and these are very highly prized.

Coco Chanel is another legendary name, and some of her creations, such as beaded 1920s cocktail dresses, appear in the salerooms today, and can still be worn. Designer clothes from the past by Molyneux, Schiaparelli, Dior, and Mary Quant often come to light when they are inherited from mothers and grandmothers, and can inspire a collection. The clothes in the closet from today's designers — Jean Muir, Vivienne Westwood, — could be the legends of tomorrow.

ABOVE *An illustration from* Art-Goût-Beauté, *July 1923, highly prized by fashion plate collectors.*

| COST | ● ● |
| OUTLOOK | ● ● ● |

RIGHT *Erté (the pseudonym of Romain de Tirtoff) was the illustrator of Paul Poiret fashion and of flamboyant theatrical costumes such as this design for* A Thousand and One Nights.

| COST | ● ● ● |
| OUTLOOK | ● ● ● ● |

ABOVE *Costume design for a dancer in* Suite Arabe *by Leon Bakst, a legendary name from the Ballets Russes.*

| COST | ● ● |
| OUTLOOK | ● ● ● |

OPPOSITE PAGE *The spirit of the racy 1920s captured on a* Vogue *cover for 1925.*

| COST | ● ● |
| OUTLOOK | ● ● |

Day Wear

AT THE BEGINNING of the century women still laced themselves into whalebone corsets. There was eventually a revolt against such restriction, first expressed in the beautiful clothes designed by Frenchman Paul Poiret. Until the end of the World War I clothes like Poiret's were only available to the very rich. Other women wore high-necked, tucked blouses and flowing, plain-colored skirts during the day. The outbreak of war in 1914 saw the adoption of shorter skirts and military style jackets, often fastened with braided frogging. As soon as the war was over, a sort of euphoric madness took over fashion. Skirts were shortened still more and necklines dropped; the bust disappeared and women tried to look more like boys than Art Nouveau odalisques.

In the 1930s the line was slim and elegant, with skirts flaring out below the knee. Synthetic rayon appeared and allowed cheap dresses to be produced. By the 1940s nylon superseded all other synthetics and revolutionized women's wear. World War II caused vast changes to fashion through shortages. Sweaters were hand-knitted from re-cycled wool and old clothes were cut down and skimpily remodeled.

The immediate postwar period brought the "New Look," pioneered by Christian Dior, which once again changed the shape of women. The androgynous look disappeared and curves came back in fashion. Every shop girl could now afford a New Look skirt and fashion was no longer the exclusive province of the well-to-do.

Clothes from the 1950s, boom years for clothing manufacturers, are among the hottest properties in fashion collecting today. There are entire auction sales devoted to them and they make a fascinating subject for collection. The trimmed down, spare lines of clothes by designers like Mary Quant followed in the 1960s — notably the mini-skirt. The mass production fashion industry took off when Barbara Hulanicki started Biba in London and designers like Bill Gibb, Ossie Clark, and Jeff Banks aimed their lines at the woman-in-the-street. Plastic became a fashionable material in its own right — shoes, boots, skirts, and coats were made of it and it was also used for trimmings on dresses. There was a lot of talk about space-age clothes in which aluminum-colored plastic was a favorite material.

ABOVE *A beige crêpe de Chine summer dress, constructed from interlocking panels linked by fagoting, possibly by Vionnet, c. 1928.*

COST	● ● ●
OUTLOOK	● ●

ABOVE *Afternoon dress of wool voile in bright kelly green was the Paris spring fashion of 1946 by Jacques Heim.*

COST	● ● ●
OUTLOOK	● ●

TOP RIGHT *Red, white, and blue mini-dress outfit by Courrèges with a Givenchy straw hat.*

| COST | ● ● ● |
| OUTLOOK | ● ● |

BELOW *Embroidered jeans jacket — street fashion in the 1980s.*

| COST | ● ● |
| OUTLOOK | ● ● ● |

ABOVE *Rock 'n' Roll fashion by Teddy Tinling: a 1950s matching shirt, shorts, and button-through skirt which could be removed for energetic dancing.*

| COST | ● ● ● |
| OUTLOOK | ● ● |

Evening Wear

ABOVE *A silk cocktail gown with three tiers of scalloped beading in silver-gray on olive green (left), and a beaded cocktail dress of ivory muslin with gold chevrons and pale blue roses (right).*

COST	● ● ●
OUTLOOK	● ● ●

THROUGHOUT HISTORY WOMEN HAVE taken the most care of their evening gowns. Evening was the time to display fashion to its best advantage.

The dawning of the 20th century saw a move away from the constricting crinoline and bustle which had held sway for almost 200 years (with only a slight interruption at the beginning of the 19th century when Directoire dresses were all the rage). It was Charles Frederick Worth, an Englishman working in Paris and the first dressmaker to put his signature on the clothes he made, who started the new trend of looser, less constricting dresses. His work was carried on by Paul Poiret who banished the corset, and during World War I the house of Lanvin began its long career.

From that point the evening dress took off in glory, progressing through Vionnet's figure-fitting, bias-cut dresses to the magnificent gowns dreamed up by Fortuny. These still sell for large sums today. Though Fortuny was born in Spain, he spent most of his working life in Venice. He was more interested in color and fabric than shape, and his gowns were so easy to wear that they could be slipped over the head and loosely belted at the waist.

Fortuny used natural dyes — hardly two pieces were ever the same color — and the tiny pleats which were his hallmark were formed by hand and set by heat. No one else, not even when using synthetic fabrics, has ever managed to make them so precisely or with such a lasting quality. To keep the pleating in place, a Fortuny gown had to be twisted like a skein of wool after wearing. Perfect for modern air travelers! The first Fortuny gown, called Delphos, was produced in 1907 and was based on the pleated chitons worn by the maidens in Greek sculpture. It was such a success that Fortuny went on making these gowns for another forty years.

Other evening dressmakers of quality were Madame Grès who worked in classically draped jersey; Patou who pioneered the longer silhouette in the 1930s; and Balenciaga who transformed the evening dress into a sheath. Courrèges then came along and hacked it off at the knees.

Wonderful old evening dresses can still be found in junk shops and auctions. Some other top names include Adrian, Schiaparelli, Rochas, and Dior. Recently there has been a move to "investment" dressing with women spending money on clothes that will in time be collectors' pieces. The dresses they wear carry the labels of St Laurent, Bill Blass, and the Emmanuels.

ABOVE *Evening dress of pale blue pleated chiffon decorated with bugles and feathers by the English designer Bill Gibb, 1977.*

COST	● ● ●
OUTLOOK	● ● ●

ABOVE *Ball gown of royal blue lace with diagonal neckline, the skirt a cone-shaped spiral with bands of sequin trimming, by Lucien Lelong, 1937.*

COST	● ● ●
OUTLOOK	● ● ●

LEFT *Evening cloak of white rayon jersey and organdy by Yuki, 1977.*

COST	● ● ●
OUTLOOK	● ●

Suits & Coats

A "WELL-CUT SUIT" is every smart woman's ideal and the desire to own such a thing dates back to the beginning of the century when fashion magazines carried line drawings of ladies dressed in long jacketed, often masculine-looking suits called "walking costumes." They were made of fine broadcloth with floor-sweeping skirts and were heavily trimmed with buttons or braiding.

These suits were figure-constricting and it was only during World War I that fashion permitted more laxity. Loosely belted suits made in tweed and based on gentlemen's shooting outfits became the fashion. Large hips were abandoned as a female ideal as far as dressmakers were concerned by 1924, and after that time suits were free to evolve into the easy-to-wear creations of Coco Chanel, a style that has never lost its popularity.

It is interesting too that the colors of suits and coats used to be rigidly confined to the more somber shades. The first hint of lightness came after World War I when beige became the most popular color, but it was said by cynics that clothing manufacturers were left with so much khaki dye that they maneuvered fashion color in order to use it up.

In the context of fashion, a coat is much more than a shield against the cold. A study of the coat through the 20th century shows it evolving from capes and cloaks to the slim-fitting Jazz Age coat with heavy borders of fur around hem and neck. The tweed coats of the 1930s were often double-breasted and adorned with rolling lapels almost like the coats worn by men. Lighter, less warm coats from the same period were fastened with a single button at the waist or were simply wide open, with the sides touching "edge to edge." The period after World War II saw a return of more military styles — perhaps for the same reason as the beige fashions of 1918 — and then camel coats in "officer style" became very fashionable.

Until recent times when animal rights activists have wakened consciences, a fur coat was the mark of a well-dressed and prosperous woman. These were made from every type of skin from rabbit to sable, including lambskin, ponyskin, and moleskin. Child movie star Shirley Temple wore a cut-down fur coat in one of her movies. Fur capes were popular for evening wear and women who could not afford a full fur coat contented themselves with fur collars and cuffs or a fur tippet, the most popular of which were made of silver foxes with the masks forming the clasp.

ABOVE *A smart geometric design of 1965. Unlike classic coat styles that may stay in fashion for most of a lifetime, this coat expressed the mood of the moment.*

COST	● ●
OUTLOOK	● ●

ABOVE *A mohair and silk tweed suit with the Chanel label, dated 1968, shows her enduring appeal.*

COST	● ● ●
OUTLOOK	● ●

TOP *Green velvet evening coat with high fur collar and tasseled ties, labeled Liberty & Co., London, c. 1915-20.*

COST	● ● ●
OUTLOOK	● ● ●

LEFT *Balenciaga wool suit: investment dressing in the 1950s.*

COST	● ● ●
OUTLOOK	● ●

ABOVE *Wartime utility clothes displayed by war-worker former mannequins, showing the original design model of a costume (left) and the mass-produced version (right).*

COST	● ●
OUTLOOK	● ● ●

Swimwear & Lingerie

SEA-BATHING WAS first considered beneficial around 1800 and ladies taking ocean dips from bathing-machines bought special bathing dresses which, even at their most voluminous, were a lot lighter than their ordinary clothes. In the beginning they went into the water attired in a skirt, a hat, stockings, and shoes but gradually sleeves became shorter, necklines lower, and daring pantaloons appeared. Mob caps and little rubber swimming shoes were worn until the 1920s when the head-hugging rubber bathing cap first appeared. In the Jazz Age swimming was all the rage among the smart set, particularly on the French Riviera, and men's and women's bathing suits with low slung belts at the hips were often attractive.

There was, however, little advance in the styling of bathing suits from 1910 until after the end of World War II when women began wearing body-fitting, almost corseted suits of elasticated material. These were often printed in bright colorful designs and were regarded as the very latest thing. Few of them have survived because the rubber perished but more endurable were the cotton swimsuits with frilly skirts and halter necks which were all the rage in the 1950s. No bathing suit ever made a bigger sensation than the bikini, that daring two-piece which looks almost puritanical today but which burst upon the world with such a shock that it was named after the Pacific island where a 1940s nuclear device was tested.

In the 19th century, lingerie, for those who could afford it, was prim and usually made of white cotton. There is still a vogue for buying and wearing 19th-century nightdresses with broderie anglaise trimming and satin ribbons, but smarter collectors now look out for pieces from the 1920s and 1930s when cami-knickers, glamorous wraps, and satin slips were all the rage. Kimonos, often heavily embroidered on silk, became fashionable; many of them were brought back from the Far East by people returning from abroad. Swansdown feathers were added to the sleeves and necklines of wraps and, though this decoration has not survived well, it added a dimension of glamour.

The growth of the artificial silk industry changed the fashion habits of poorer women because, even without a lot of money, they could buy pretty nightdresses, slim-line dressing gowns overprinted in bright geometric patterns, and scraps of flimsy underwear. Women who a few years before would never have dreamed of spending money on underwear, found the items offered in large department stores too tempting to miss.

ABOVE *Slip and French panties — early examples of a synthetic fabric being used for lingerie in the 1940s.*

COST	● ●
OUTLOOK	● ●

ABOVE *Slip of art silk and lace from the 1920s.*

COST	● ●
OUTLOOK	● ●

ABOVE *Pink moiré boudoir gown of watered silk edged with blue satin (left), and a goffered silk kimono (right), mid-1920s.*

COST	● ● ●
OUTLOOK	● ●

ABOVE *Nightdress of broderie anglaise probably from the turn of the century, when a lady's maid could take care of the ironing.*

COST	● ●
OUTLOOK	● ●

ABOVE *New bathing fashions for 1935, designed by Forma and photographed on a rooftop in London's West End.*

COST	● ●
OUTLOOK	● ●

LEFT *Nightwear of the 1920s: the lady has a lime green, lace-trimmed satin nightdress and negligee with matching lace boudoir cap, and the gentleman wears pink silk pajamas.*

COST	● ● ●
OUTLOOK	● ●

Watches

WRIST WATCHES ARE a development of the 20th century; previously only fob or pocket watches were worn.

Some of the most attractive watches from a collector's point of view are the slim, elegant models produced in the 1930s by manufacturers including Rolex, Patek Philippe, Piquet, Cartier, Jaeger Le Coultre, and Movado. Buyers should check that the watch cases are not worn or dented.

The most desirable watch is the Rolex Oyster, worn as a sign of affluence ever since it was first produced in 1927. The Oyster was the first weather- and climate-proof watch and its superior workmanship and reliability make it an excellent buy. The older a watch is the better from a collector's point of view. Rolexes were made in 9 ct gold, 18 ct gold, striped gold, silver and stainless steel. Strangely, a lady's Rolex Oyster will sell for only half as much as a man's and, in fact, over the whole spectrum, women's watches are all priced lower than men's.

In the 1930s and 1940s cocktail watches, worn on the wrist or as brooches, became very popular with women and were produced studded with diamonds or, in the cheaper versions, set with marquisites. If they are of attractive Art Deco designs and the work of good makers like Patek Philippe, they can be very valuable.

Some one-of-a-kind watches demand enormous prices when they come up for sale. A prime example is a silver aviator's watch by Longines, called the Charles Lindbergh Navigating Model. Lindbergh, who flew across the Atlantic in 1927, had only a compass and a standard watch to guide him, and he had the idea of a watch that would indicate both Greenwich Time and the corresponding hour angle. His designs were shown to Longines who produced the watch.

OPPOSITE LEFT *Cocktail watch with cover from the 1950s.*

COST	● ●	
OUTLOOK	● ●	

OPPOSITE CENTER *Watch in enameled metal case, 1930.*

COST	● ● ●	
OUTLOOK	● ● ●	

OPPOSITE RIGHT *Gold and steel Swiss watch, 1920.*

COST	● ●	
OUTLOOK	● ●	

TOP RIGHT *"Santos" sports watch made of stainless steel and gold, Cartier, 1978. This model immediately became a classic.*

COST	● ●	
OUTLOOK	● ● ● ●	

BELOW RIGHT *Collection of Lip designed watches from the 1950s and 1960s.*

COST	● ●	
OUTLOOK	● ●	

RIGHT *Lady's watch of white gold and diamond, 1930s.*

COST	● ●	
OUTLOOK	● ● ●	

FAR RIGHT *La Vérité cocktail watch, 1950.*

COST	● ●	
OUTLOOK	● ●	

Accessories

SOME OF THE MOST beautiful accessories come from the Art Nouveau period: silver-topped parasols; chain-link belts such as those designed for Liberty & Co. by Alexander Knox; enameled hatpins; finely wrought buttons of bone, silver, or horn; buckles enameled and shaped like butterflies with interlinking wings; evening headdresses with aigrette feathers set in jeweled bands. Luxury items in their time, they are still expensive today, though modest collectors can search out more everyday items, such as scarves. During World War II when it was difficult to buy hats, women took to wearing headscarves which in time became a fashion. Even the Queen of England wore a headscarf and she wears them still. Firms like Jacqmar produced scarves in cotton and silk, some designed by famous artists or to mark special events. They had a fine range in silk, redesigned annually to commemorate each horse that won the English Derby for several years after the War. These are well worth collecting.

Also being collected now are buttons from the 1930s and 1940s, especially early plastic ones. These can still be found in boxes of mixed buttons which turn up in rummage and second-hand sales. Buttons were characteristic of their period and some elegant designs were produced, particularly geometrical Art Deco ones.

Artificial flowers were extremely popular from the 1920s until the 1950s when they were worn on hats or as corsage decorations. They were made in stiffened cotton, synthetic, or silk, and during World War II, lapel flowers were made from dried leaves and beech mast, sprayed with gold or silver paint.

Hats used to be absolutely essential wear for smartness and the cheeky little hat was a mark of high fashion in the 1930s, especially the ones made in fine pliable straw decorated with dyed ostrich feathers. Especially popular with accessory collectors today are small cocktail hats made of felt or stiffened silk, often with eye veils. Some 1950s examples were made of plastic leaves, like beetles' wings or jet, or stitched all over with beading and sequins.

Any collector building up a representative selection of the accessories of the 1960s should not forget to include a pair of white plastic platform boots and a Biba feather boa. Remember that to be collectible, accessories should be representative of that period, in good condition, of good quality, and well designed.

ABOVE *Art Deco purses and shoes from an era of high quality, expensive accessories.*

COST	● ●
OUTLOOK	● ●

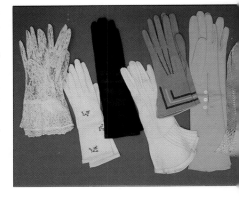

ABOVE *Gloves in leather, cotton, and nylon from 1920s-1980s.*

COST	● ●
OUTLOOK	● ●

ABOVE *Italian shoes with the stiletto heels that aroused strong criticism in the 1950s.*

COST	● ●
OUTLOOK	● ●

ABOVE *Hats — mostly for weddings. Left to right: sequined, U.S.A., 1940; straw, 1960s; and spotted, 1940s.*

COST	● ●
OUTLOOK	● ●

ABOVE *Corsage, hair, and hat ornaments from the 1930s and 1940s.*

COST	● ●
OUTLOOK	● ●

BELOW *To brighten the eye of button collectors: buttons ranging from 1900s jet to 1950s plastic.*

COST	●
OUTLOOK	● ●

A large Steiff German teddy bear,
c. 1904.

CHAPTER NINE

Toys

BEARS & DOLLS

DOLLHOUSES

TRAINS

CARS

BOARD GAMES & PUZZLES

BOYS' TOYS

WOODEN TOYS

Introduction

THE NURSERY OF THE 1900s was a very different place from that of the previous century. Nannies were rarer and mothers had a more direct hand in raising their children. The birthrate fell. Two children, one of each sex, were considered to be the perfect family and this ideal pair could be indulged and lavished with gifts by people with money to spend.

Even during the years of the Depression, spending on children was high. Toy shops opened their doors in every town, and in the cities, vast toy emporia like F. A. O. Schwartz were packed with toys and diversions of all sorts for the young. The age of commercialism began. At Christmas, Santa Claus appeared in stores, solemnly listening to the many requests of young children. Parents who had themselves experienced the rigors of a 19th century childhood were eager to make things easier for their sons and daughters. The age of "spoiling" had arrived.

Manufacturers were quick to respond to this new market, and they courted their customers with toys that reflected every new aspect of modern life — toy cars, trains powered by electricity that could whizz around their rails, talking dolls, dollhouses with up-to-date furniture and real lighting . . . nothing was too good for the children.

Bisque character dolls by Kammer and Reinhardt, German, c. 1911.

Meccano set No. 8, designed for future engineers.

Tinplate and wind-up buses from the 1950s by Wells Brimtoys, London.

A rocking horse — the pride of any nursery — 1969.

Four-stack battleship with wind-up mechanism, by Bing of Germany, c. 1912.

Model to delight the train enthusiast: American Flyer, 1915.

Hornby Dublo train set.

Prewar airplanes by Dinky in their original boxes, which adds to their value.

"MacFoo" — painted tinplate motorbike and rider with wind-up mechanism, c. 1955.

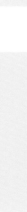

Bright and jolly toys designed by Rylands, 1970.

Japanese lunar module for the collector of space-age toys.

Bears & Dolls

THE TEDDY BEAR is not only the most successful toy ever manufactured but it also marks a change in the popular attitude toward children. The exquisite dolls made in the 18th and 19th centuries were to be looked at but rarely handled, whereas a teddy bear could be cuddled, scuffed, dribbled over, and generally loved by all children. Teddy bears brought liberation to the nursery, and there are few bears around today that do not show some evidence of childhood play.

There are various stories of how those plush-coated bears got their name: the most likely concerns President Teddy Roosevelt. It seems that while on a hunting trip in 1902, the President could not bring himself to shoot a bear cub and a newspaper cartoonist recorded his clemency in a drawing. Roosevelt adopted the image of a cuddly little bear as his own and when his daughter got married in 1906, the wedding breakfast tables were decorated with tiny bears made by the Steiff toy company.

Margarete Steiff, a crippled German toymaker, had been making toy bears since around 1900 but the teddy bear craze was to transform her life into that of a business magnate. Her factory produced a vast number of bears in several different styles, including an unnerving looking one with two heads, and all sizes from 6in (15cm) to 24in (60cm) long. Early Steiff bears made before 1910 are very valuable and are distinguishable by their humped backs, long muzzles, elongated arms and feet, short legs, and long bodies. They were stuffed with wood shavings and covered in plush. Most had a growler and, if it still works, their present-day price is sky-high.

Around the time of World War I the design was modified. The hump disappeared, the muzzle shrank, and the bears began to look more human in shape — a good psychological move that made them even more endearing to the public. After 1920 the stuffing was changed to kapok.

Buyers could always tell a Steiff bear because Margarete had the good business sense to mark her products with distinctive buttons in their left ears. Today some battle-weary bears have lost their buttons but their general shape and style are still a guide to whether they are genuine Steiff models. The bear boom of course brought in many competitors, among them the Bing and Schuco factories whose bears are also collected today, though not so avidly as Steiff ones. (Schuco extended its range to appeal to adults, with tiny teddies in bright crimson and violet plush whose stomachs opened to reveal powder compacts or perfume bottles.)

In the U.S., the Jacal Toy Co. started to make teddy bears, as did many manufacturers in Britain, including Chad Valley and Merrythought. British bears nearly always growled and were squatter than American ones.

The most exquisite dolls of the 18th and 19th centuries were not made for children but for ladies of fashion who dressed them in pretty clothes. They were too good for little girls to play with, and children had to be content with homemade rag dolls or roughly carved wooden ones. But, in the 20th century, with people's attitudes toward children changing, nothing was too good for them, and even parents with little spare money would scrimp and save to give their daughter a pretty doll for Christmas. To cater to this new demand, doll manufacturers introduced many different models. Margarete Steiff also made soft dolls in felt, often caricatures of policemen or sailors. They were distinguished by the left ear button also found in her bears.

Another German doll maker, Kathe Kruse, made soft cloth dolls stuffed with sand. They still had painted heads because the long-established manufacture of dolls' heads by firms like Jumeau was still going strong. These pliant, tactile dolls proved very popular and in Italy Madame Scavini started a firm called Lenci which is still making beautiful felt dolls with dancing eyes. In England, Deans, a firm that made rag books for children, also extended its range to dolls.

The doll industry took off in America before 1900, but demand from consumers increased to an unprecedented extent after World War I. There had long been a link with what was happening in Europe because American designers were responsible for many of the dolls' heads manufactured in Germany during the 19th century. The first American innovation was Phonograph dolls, patented by Edison, which were produced by a workforce of over 500 people by 1900; then, in 1920, came the Kewpie doll with its rubber body designed by Ernesto Peruggi for the Manhattan Toy and Doll Manufacturing Co.

In England, Chad Valley made dolls with composition bodies and engaged artist Mabel Lucie Attwell to design for them. They also produced a range of soft dolls and puppets, including a set of Snow White and the Seven Dwarfs which was very much in vogue in the 1930s. About the same time the firm Merrythought launched its popular range, extending from toy parrots to puppets and pierrots.

In spite of the rigors of the Depression, the making and selling of dolls boomed. Little girls treasured dolls modeled on Shirley Temple, chubby babies, or the princesses Elizabeth and Margaret Rose. Dolls were available in all sizes and price ranges, but one doll maker who aimed her products at the luxury market was Norah Wellings. She made elaborately dressed dolls that were sold on board the Cunard liners crossing the Atlantic. Doll making is still a booming industry and America's Cabbage Patch dolls, which are exported worldwide, could well be the collectibles of the future.

LEFT *Two blond plush teddy bears, one with the Steiff metal button in the left ear, c. 1908.*

COST	● ● ● ●
OUTLOOK	● ●

RIGHT *Rare Steiff doll with black boot button eyes, c. 1905.*

COST	● ● ●
OUTLOOK	● ●

ABOVE LEFT *Two Sasha dolls by Frido Ltd., 1966.*

COST	● ●
OUTLOOK	● ●

LEFT *Action Man and his space clothes, 1979.*

COST	● ●
OUTLOOK	● ●

ABOVE *Dolls by Norah Wellings were sold on board the Cunard liners crossing the Atlantic in the 1930s.*

COST	● ●
OUTLOOK	● ●

Dollhouses

IN THE 1930s, while the owner-occupier boom was taking hold of adults, children were also into property, and the sale of dollhouses boomed.

Victorian nurseries had had their dollhouses, developed from the elegant toy houses of the 18th century which were usually played with by adults. Victorian parents looked on a dollhouse as an instructional toy, and it was meant to teach little girls the essentials of household management. In the 20th century, however, the instructional side became less important and dollhouses were bought to be played with.

Just as toy trains enthral fathers as much as their sons, dollhouses fascinate little girls and their mothers. Queen Mary, wife of King George V, was a dollhouse addict and had a beautiful one in Windsor Castle for which she was continually collecting new pieces. She made it the palace of dollhouses.

Sometimes fathers made dollhouses for their daughters, but there was also a thriving industry producing everything from cheap cardboard versions to solidly built reproductions of Tudor-style villas, with hollyhocks painted along the front wall and electric lights in every room.

Some of the French houses were faithful scale models of Parisian mansions, complete with elevators that worked. In the 1960s there was a big upsurge in dollhouse making, and craftsmen turned out reproductions of period houses, especially from the Georgian period, some of which were extremely expensive.

The furnishing of a dollhouse can be a lifetime hobby, as Queen Mary proved. Manufacturers produced a wide range of pieces from cheap bakelite armchairs to expensive scale models of good-quality furniture. It was possible to buy a whole world in miniature: pianos, pictures to hang on the wall, radios, bathroom suites, tiny mirrors, and plaster legs of lamb to put on scrubbed kitchen tables. The inhabitants of the dollhouse could also be purchased — mothers, fathers, babies in carriages, and maids in stiff white aprons. With dollhouse furniture collecting now a boom area, toy furniture is being made in Taiwan, Korea, and Hong Kong as well as in Europe and America. Some pieces of good-quality toy furniture bring higher prices than the real thing.

OPPOSITE FAR LEFT *Dollhouse of the 1920s, complete with backyard swing — a child's play version of a desirable family home in the English suburbs.*

COST	●●
OUTLOOK	●●●

OPPOSITE LEFT *Dollhouse, c. 1900, with blue painted gabled roof and a central turret. The outside is lithographed in cream with a "brick" decoration.*

COST	●●
OUTLOOK	●●●

ABOVE *American dollhouse, c. 1900, by Bliss Manufacturing Company, made of wood with lithographed paper decorations.*

COST	●●●
OUTLOOK	●●

Trains

COST	● ●
OUTLOOK	● ● ●

THE GROWTH OF TRANSPORTATION in the 20th century soon made its mark on the toy world. When the century began the train was already a well-established form of transportation, and fine models were made in France and Germany by Marklin, Gebruder Bing, Georges Carette, Ernst Plank, and Jean Schoenner. The idea was taken up in England by Bassett-Lowke who started manufacturing toy trains in a Northampton factory early in the century and continued in production until the 1950s. But the toy train maker *par excellence* was Frank Hornby, inventor of Meccano, who in 1907 started producing the trains that were to make his name famous.

When the Flying Scotsman traveled at 100 mph in 1934, models could not be made quickly enough to satisfy the demand. The train was reproduced by Bassett-Lowke in Gauge 0 and could be bought as a wind-up model or powered by electricity. Model train enthusiasts, fathers as well as sons, bought thousands of miles of rails and countless boxes of lineside equipment, much of it produced by Bing.

BELOW *Victorian engines — models which celebrate the great days of the railroad.*

COST	● ●
OUTLOOK	● ● ●

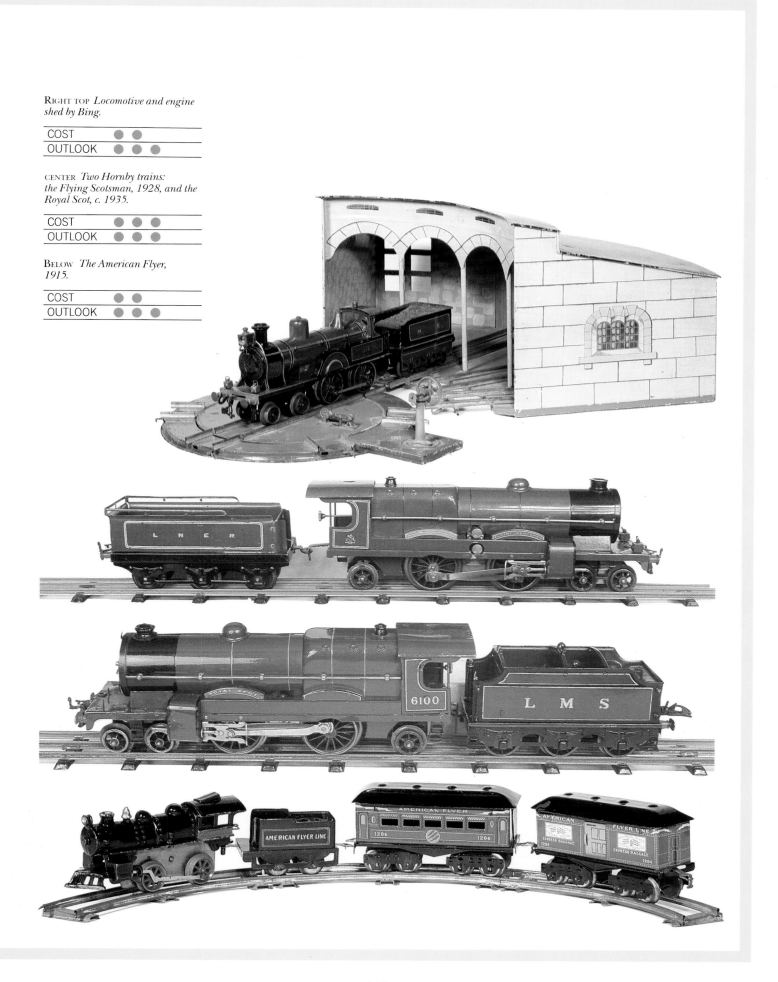

RIGHT TOP *Locomotive and engine shed by Bing.*

COST	● ●	
OUTLOOK	● ●	●

CENTER *Two Hornby trains: the Flying Scotsman, 1928, and the Royal Scot, c. 1935.*

COST	● ●	●
OUTLOOK	● ●	●

BELOW *The American Flyer, 1915.*

COST	● ●	
OUTLOOK	● ●	●

Cars

MOTORING MANIA also had its impact on the world of juvenilia. Tinplate toy manufacturers were early in the game with wind-up models of the 1907 Carette open tourer and Lehmann's tourer cars, and the 1930s saw a great expansion in model making. Chad Valley's wind-up racing cars had a huge sale, as did Schuco wind-up autos, and in 1933 Frank Hornby had another good idea when he introduced Dinky toys. The name meant "neat" or "tiny," and the original intention was to make accessories for train sets, but the range grew to encompass all sorts of transportation.

ABOVE *Vintage limousine with wind-up mechanism by Carette, German, c. 1912.*

COST	● ● ● ●
OUTLOOK	● ● ● ●

The first Dinky toys were a tank, two sports cars, a tractor, a truck, and delivery van, and the models were modestly priced — delivery vans cost ten cents each — but now, if they are still painted with advertising signs for Oxo, Hovis, or Fry's Chocolate, they are worth hundreds of dollars. They were cast in heavy lead alloy with metal wheels but by World War II they had become lighter and the wheels had white rubber tires that wore away or went flat, an infallible sign of authenticity. The range expanded to include road signs, farm animals, and wayside buildings.

Postwar Dinky vehicles had black rubber tires, and new lines were produced every year, even a model of the Beatles' "Yellow Submarine." In 1980, after delighting generations of children, Dinky ceased production; however, in 1988 they started up again, reproducing their old models.

Collectors should seek out models in their original boxes and as near mint condition as possible, though even well-worn prewar models sell well. Other model cars worth collecting are Matchbox, Lesney's Yesteryear range, Corgi, Rio, Tenko, and Spot. (Frank Hornby's Meccano sets should be complete, not rusted or worn, and in their original boxes, to be collectible.)

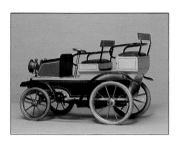

ABOVE *Rare tinplate station wagon by Bing in fine condition, handpainted in strong colors, with wind-up mechanism driving the rear axle.*

COST	● ● ● ● ●
OUTLOOK	● ● ● ●

ABOVE *Dinky Supertoys: Heinz 57 varieties Bedford delivery truck, and Ever Ready Guy delivery truck, both in original boxes.*

COST	● ●
OUTLOOK	● ● ● ●

LEFT *"MacFoo": German wind-up motorbike and rider, c. 1955.*

COST	● ●
OUTLOOK	● ● ● ●

Dinky airplanes

Probably the most sought-after aircraft for any Dinky collector is No. 992, the Avro Vulcan. This model of the most famous of the RAF Delta Wing Bombers was produced between 1955 and 1956 and differed from others in that it was finished in silver and made entirely of aluminum.

The bulk of the 500 or so produced were sold in North America for just $1.40 each but so far very few have come to light. Find one of these Dinky Super Toys complete with its original box, which is extremely rare, and you could reasonably expect it to bring about $2500 at auction.

Board Games & Puzzles

IN THE PERIOD between the two world wars, parents' attitudes toward their children continued to soften. The old belief, particularly in upper-and middle-class homes, that children should be rarely seen and hardly ever heard was gradually swept away, and it was common for a family to spend their spare time together. Some of the favorite ways of spending an evening were listening to the family radio or playing games.

To cater to the demand a huge selection of games was available, for example, cheap packs of Happy Family cards, board games like Snakes and Ladders, expensive ivory and ebony checker sets, and Bagatelle, a wooden frame set with a network of pegs around which players had to push silver balls with a round-tipped stick.

There was a whole new industry dreaming up and producing games that adults could play with children. Fretwork machines were sold in their thousands to fathers who wanted to cut their own jigsaw puzzles and paper-making companies

like Waddingtons opened puzzle departments. Philmar was another producer of a wide range of puzzles. Some of the favorite scenes for these puzzles during the Depression were idyllic gardens with white doves roosting on the roofs of thatched houses and roses burgeoning around the doors.

Snakes and Ladders, an old Indian game revised for the benefit of 20th-century families, was one of the best-selling board games. But the man who made a fortune out of the game-playing passion was an American named Charles Darrow, an unemployed heating engineer, who in 1933 dreamed up the idea of Monopoly. His first board was based on the streets of his home town, Atlantic City, New Jersey. Later, when Monopoly was imported to Britain, the names of Mayfair, Marylebone, and St. Pancras appeared around the famous board, which, still sold in its original box design, is the biggest-selling board game ever invented, even outselling Trivial Pursuit.

Disneyana

Few people would seek to deny that the fourth son of Elias and Flora Disney, born on Sunday, December 5, 1901, at 1249 Tripp Avenue, Chicago, has made the greatest contribution to the world of fun and laughter.
Success on a small scale came for him at nine when a number of his cartoons were published in his school magazine at McKinley High. From newspaper delivery boy to handyman at a jelly factory, he eventually became a cartoonist on the *Kansas City Star* when he was just nineteen. After one or two setbacks Mickey Mouse appeared in 1928, and the rest is history.
The full commercial qualities of his characters were seen from the beginning and toys from

this era can now be worth amazing money. Only recently a Mickey Mouse organ grinder, just 6in (15cm) long, made by Distler in 1930, sold for well over $3500.
The market for Disney products has always been universal, and enthusiastic and eager collectors of Disneyana can be confident of a wise investment.

OPPOSITE TOP *Puzzle made of plywood by Chad Valley, 1940s.*

COST	● ●
OUTLOOK	● ●

OPPOSITE CENTER *Building block game from the 1920s, enjoyed by adults too.*

COST	● ●
OUTLOOK	● ●

Money banks

Most early money banks are made of metal; many have a mechanical function, and most still work. The first patent for a cast-iron mechanical bank was taken out by J. Hall on December 21, 1869, for his Excelsior Bank and this was still being made well into the 20th century. In the simplest kind, a coin placed on the hand of a Negro figure passes through the mouth into the body of the bank when a lever is activated. Others shoot an apple off the head of William Tell's son, while yet another causes a dog to leap through a hoop and deposit the coin from its mouth into a barrel. Occasionally, however, a hitherto unknown example comes onto the market, such as one featuring a girl skipping, which sold for an amazing $14,000.

LEFT *The box labels of Chad Valley games, 1924, are collectible.*

COST	
OUTLOOK	

RIGHT *Monopoly — the best-selling game of all.*

COST	
OUTLOOK	

Boys' Toys

THE YEAR 1900 marked the height of the golden age of the Empire as far as the British were concerned. They thought of themselves as masters of the world, undefeated in battle, and military values were glorified. It is not surprising that the manufacture of toy soldiers proved to be such a success when the firm of William Britain launched itself on the market at this time of supreme confidence.

Toy soldiers had been made in Germany by people like Heinrichsen and Heyd half a century before, but Britain's recognized the mass-market potential if they could manufacture their toys cheaply enough. They achieved this by casting their figures in lead and turning each line out in the thousands.

They set out to reproduce every regiment in the British Army first, and, that achieved, extended their range to foreign forces. Among their figures were cavalry men, infantry men, bandsmen, gunners, sailors, and men of the Camel Corps. Today the rarest sets from this period are those dating from the Boer War and certain sets of cavalry. All their early castings are valuable, however, especially if they have not been repainted by some over-enthusiastic collector. Early ones can be spotted because they were mounted on circular bases, and if the base is stamped "William Britain," that dates it before 1912. Between 1912 and 1917 the mark was "Britain's Ltd." and after that, until the firm ceased production in 1953, "England" was added.

Between the wars, lead was used less and soldiers were produced in composition mixtures with names like Lineol and Elastolin, which stood up better to handling. Production was sustained in restricted numbers during World War II, and one of the rarest sets from this period is that of the Royal Horse Artillery, which was produced around 1940.

Infinite expertise and ingenuity has gone into making mechanical toys for a couple of hundred years. Collectors pay astronomical prices for battleships, tinplate cars, and trains produced by firms like Marklin or Bing but, in the mid-20th century, wind-up mechanisms were largely replaced by electric motors running on batteries. This brought about a switch from the old toy-making centers of Germany and France to Japan, and some of the lines produced there have turned into collectors' pieces only a few years after their debut on the market. Transformer toys from the mid 1980s are worth collecting now with an eye to the future because of the ingenuity of the idea. Japanese space toys such as the Nomura "Walking Astroman" are popular with collectors. Wind-up or battery toys from the 1960s are soaring in price and although the Japanese were the chief manufacturers, look out for those made in the U.S., such as the Charlie Weaver bartender who shakes a cocktail shaker while smoke comes out of his ears.

BELOW *Tinplate mechanical angler, with moving wind-up rod, by F. Martin; French, c. 1900.*

| COST | ● ● |
| OUTLOOK | ● ● ● |

BELOW LEFT AND RIGHT *Royal Air Force Colour Party in Britain's set No. 2171.*

| COST | ● ● |
| OUTLOOK | ● ● ● |

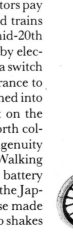

BELOW *Printed and painted tinplate motorcyclist — Echo EPL 725 — with a wind-up mechanism; Lehmann, c. 1901.*

| COST | ● ● |
| OUTLOOK | ● ● ● |

Robots

Toyland was first invaded by robots in the 1950s and, as you might guess, over 90 percent were made in Japan.
These colorful tinplate mechanical men and other related space toys with their numerous battery-operated talents were an immediate success. They were able to perform hitherto undreamed-of feats, many combining more than one action — walking, talking, turning, shooting, flashing lights while rotating at a dizzying speed, and so on.
Demand was high in the 1960s and the manufacturers entered a golden age of production. In 1970, however, production of the well-loved tinplate models was abandoned in favor of plastic but these were not nearly as pleasing, nor as popular. Names to look for are Lilliput, Linemar, Alps Shoji, Horikawa the Attacking Martian, Mighty 8 Robot, Yoshiyo, and Mr. Atomic Robot. Most of these demand hundreds of dollars, but with the current interest we could soon be seeing the $2000-plus spaceman.

ABOVE LEFT *German lead soldiers and accessories.*

| COST | ●● | |
| OUTLOOK | ●●● | |

ABOVE *Britain's Royal Horse Artillery, Set No. 1339, with 39A box. In 1988 20,000 model soldiers — mostly Britain's — sold at an auction for prices ranging from $35 to $8500.*

| COST | ●● | |
| OUTLOOK | ●●● | |

ABOVE *Britain's set No. 1450 — Royal Army Medical Corps — c. 1940.*

| COST | ●● | |
| OUTLOOK | ●●● | |

BELOW *Britain's Regimental Models of recent date: 1970s.*

| COST | ● | |
| OUTLOOK | ●●● | |

Wooden Toys

ABOVE *An English rocking horse, 1910.*

COST	● ● ●
OUTLOOK	● ● ●

THE EARLIEST TOYS were made of wood or bundles of rags. Carved pieces of wood made into children's playthings in early times have survived and dolls in particular, especially those dating from the 16th and 17th centuries, make a great deal of money at auction or in antique shops. Some of them were finely made, with articulated limbs. They were not miniature children, but when new they were dressed like fashionable belles of the period in silks and satins. They were never intended to be handled in the nursery for they were the playthings of ladies who amused themselves dressing their dolls in the latest modes. Simpler dolls were also made of wood and the few that have survived often look battered and much handled by their young owners.

Wood was a good medium for children's toys because it was difficult to destroy. If polished it would not harm the child who played with it and it could be painted in bright colors. Tops, spinning wheels, building blocks, and cutouts of animals pulled along on wooden wheels were, and still are, great favorites. Modern wooden toys are often designed as educational aids for teaching children manual dexterity and the interrelation of shapes and figures. One of the best known manufacturers is Brio of Sweden, trendsetters in educational toys. Chad Valley and Triang also made wooden toys.

More sophisticated wooden toys include dollhouses, some of which were very detailed and full of lovely furniture. At Wallington Hall in Northumberland, England, there is a wonderful display of dollhouses and furniture dating from the 18th century to the present day. It is worth traveling a long way to see them.

Also made of wood are Noah's Arks, a particular favorite with children in the early part of the century. Until the advent of plastic, wood was also used as the medium for toy theaters and castles.

The wooden rocking horse is an embellishment for any nursery, both as a piece of decoration and a plaything. The best are still being made by skilled craftsmen and prices are very high. Any child who is given a dapple-gray rocking horse with a long tail and a red saddle has something to remember for the rest of his or her life.

Though not strictly a toy, fairground or carousel horses might be included along with rocking horses because they both have the same fanciful appearance. These horses are among the greatest hits in the collecting world and good examples go for five figure sums.

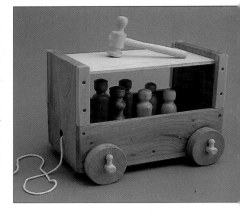

ABOVE *A model bus designed by R. & W.S. Green for Crowdys Wood.*

COST	● ●
OUTLOOK	● ● ● ●

ABOVE *German wooden toys — all very collectible.*

COST	● ●		
OUTLOOK	●	●	● ●

LEFT *A painted spinning top and rocking clown, made in 1978.*

COST	● ●		
OUTLOOK	●	●	● ●

The Beatles' Sgt. Pepper album cover, 1967.

Sound & Image

Introduction

IT IS NOT AN EXAGGERATION to say that the motion picture was one of the greatest influences on 20th-century life and culture. It helped create the modern world as we know it.

The first movies were simple and were regarded as passing fads until D.W. Griffith, a young American film maker, figured out how to use methods of pictorial emphasis like the close-up, the cutback, and the fade-out. The debut of *Ben Hur* in 1907 heralded a New Age and the magic of movies helped to cast aside barriers imposed by language and culture. Stars such as Clark Gable and Jean Harlow were known to people who had never left their own neighborhood.

To collect old movies or movie memorabilia is to collect the story of the 20th century. The movies themselves are particularly valuable and after a long period when many were neglected and allowed to rot away, it is fortunate that they are now being gathered together in movie museums.

It is not only the work of professional moviemakers that is valuable; many "home movies" made from the early part of the century onward are prized. No era in history has been able to experience such immediacy in its recollection. Thanks to newsreels and amateur moviemakers we can see what our local town or village looked like when our grandparents were alive. We can see what the Kaiser, Lenin, Hitler, and other people of historical significance really looked like. Film summons them up for us as if in real life.

The movies also created new styles of architecture, clothing, interior decoration, popular music, and graphic art. Movie posters were works of art displayed on sidewalk billboards to attract the customers. The music played as background sound tracks or to punctuate the stories enacted on celluloid was hummed and whistled by people thousands of miles away from Hollywood. The movie theaters themselves where audiences sat rapt night after night were palaces in a new style.

The age of the movies has created a huge collecting field from clothes to sheet music, posters to star magazines, pin-up pictures to celluloid records. Because it is vast and inexhaustible, enthusiasts soon specialize and they can be seen at auctions and yard sales, sifting through postcards or racks of records, browsing over old movie magazines, bidding for cans of film, or enthusing over Disney prints. Treasures can turn up at any time and any place.

West End Revue *cover by Alphonse Mucha with all the elements of Art Nouveau.*

Picture Post — *the British news magazine whose superb photographs are still remembered today.*

Unusual Beatles memorabilia — silk stockings in a box — 1960s.

Poster for "Eightpence a Mile" revue at the Alhambra Theatre, 1913.

Program for the premiere of the silent film The Merry Widow, 1925.

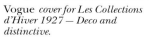

Vogue cover for Les Collections d'Hiver 1927 — Deco and distinctive.

Advertisement for Week-End cigarettes which appeared in French Vogue of June 1935.

Jolly vacation postcard by Donald McGill.

Flix movie magazine cover — 1950s.

"Guinness for Strength" poster.

Yellow Submarine celluloid: John Lennon and a Pepperlander, c. 1967.

The Sony Walkman that makes it possible to listen to music wherever you go.

The Face — magazine of young 1980s culture.

Pop Memorabilia

ONE OF THE MOST astonishing developments of the collecting world in recent years has been the huge prices people are prepared to pay for items connected with pop idols, particularly the Beatles, although Elvis Presley, Rod Stewart, and Eric Clapton are also high in the collector's favor.

Manuscripts of music, scraps of paper with poetry scribbled by John Lennon, photographs, fan letters, programs, leaflets, and concert posters relating to those artists all bring premium prices. Signed photographs are popular, but the most expensive are those signed with a personal dedication because, as in the case of movie stars, demand was so great that signatures were often forged by staff members. There is a premium on personal photographs, especially the pictures taken of the Beatles by Astrid Kircher in Hamburg in 1960. Home movies of the Beatles in their off-duty hours are also among the most valuable items of memorabilia.

There was also a huge industry specifically catering for pop stars' fans. There were cheap china mugs printed with photographs of the Beatles that now bring many times their original cost. There were stockings with the Beatles' signatures woven into the tops. A cotton dress printed with the Beatles' pictures that was worn by an usherette at the premiere of *A Hard Day's Night* is now very expensive because the girl was enterprising enough to ask all four of the pop stars to sign it for her. Top prices are paid for grinning plaster effigies with nodding heads of the four boys, for tins of Beatles talc by Margo of Mayfair, for watches with the Apple logo, for ashtrays, books, magazines, badges — the list is endless.

ABOVE *A good signed photograph of The Beatles in their famous gray suits, heads peeping around a door.*

COST	● ●
OUTLOOK	● ● ●

ABOVE *Important early photograph of John Lennon, George Harrison, and Stuart Sutcliffe on a truck, taken by Astrid Kirchherr.*

COST	● ●
OUTLOOK	● ● ● ●

ABOVE *Mustang Guitar by Fender, reputed to have belonged to Jimi Hendrix, complete with its own history and Leatherette case; c. 1964.*

COST	● ● ●
OUTLOOK	● ●

Equally important from a collecting point of view is Elvis Presley, who was also marketed on a vast scale by an industry that turned out things for fans to buy. Anything relating to "The King" demands a high price today.

This adulation of performers is not new, although the sky-high prices people are prepared to pay is a more recent development. Charlie Chaplin, who died in 1977, had his own marketing and licensing business during the height of his stardom which vetted, and took a percentage of, all memorabilia sold in his likeness or with his name. But even the business-minded Chaplin would have been surprised to learn that in 1986 an old pair of his boots, a bowler hat, and a cane that he had once carried, sold for almost $130,000 at auction.

ABOVE *Patek Philippe gold wristwatch in working condition that belonged to Elvis Presley around 1971 and was presented by him to someone who treated him for a sore throat.*

| COST | ● ● ● |
| OUTLOOK | ● ● |

BELOW *Rare original poster for The Who at The Marquee, Wardour Street, London, November 1964.*

| COST | ● ● |
| OUTLOOK | ● ● ● |

Beatlemania

Tens of thousands of items are available on the "fabulous four" who dominated popular music and youth culture for the best part of a decade. For the enthusiast today the hard decision is not so much what to collect but rather what not to collect. Of particular interest are those items more personally identified with the super-group such as an autographed Cavern Club membership book for 1961, which can command as much as $850. Even more sought after would be a signed Royal Variety Performance program, such as one that was recently sold for well over $1700.

But for really amazing money the handwritten lyrics of "Imagine" by John Lennon, on the reverse of a hotel bill from Majorca, dated "20/4/71," will command over $12,000, while Paul McCartney's upright piano of about 1902 sold for $17,000.

ABOVE *Polka dot cotton dress with portrait heads of all four Beatles and a guitar — as worn by usherettes at the Granada Theatre, Bedford, for a Beatles concert.*

| COST | ● ● ● |
| OUTLOOK | ● ● |

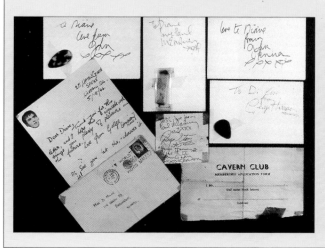

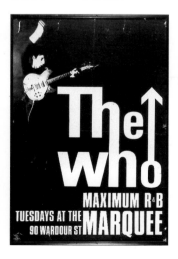

Movie Memorabilia

AN OLD BOWLER HAT, a cane, and a pair of misshapen boots can be worth a fortune, if they happen to have belonged to Charlie Chaplin. Association with movie stars sends the price of items under the hammer soaring.

Such items are not easily come by. Sometimes they are given by movie magazines as prizes; the black lace blouse Marilyn Monroe wore in the film *Bus Stop* in 1956 was won in this way. The blouse of acid green gauze overlaid with lace was sold recently at auction for around $12,000, more than double its estimated price.

Movie photographs are easily acquired; pictures of the stars were sent out by their press agents, and the photograph market became flooded with signed photographs sent to fans. There is now a growing interest in this field of collecting,

prices doubling for good-quality items in the last few years and there is every sign this upward trend will continue.

The popularity of the movie star is the first factor to affect the price achieved — Charlie Chaplin, Laurel & Hardy, Judy Garland, Rudolph Valentino, Mary Pickford, Clark Gable, and Errol Flynn are all top favorites.

Photographs with a genuine personal dedication are worth the most. Many signatures are not genuine: they were copied by machine or reproduced on the negative. The work of outstanding photographers, such as Man Ray, Baron, and Cecil Beaton, is also always in demand. Photographs of the movie star who became President, Ronald Reagan sell for around $85 today, outdone by Rudolph Valentino, whose signed photographs are rare and sell for around $850.

LEFT *Movie photograph of 1930s heartthrob Errol Flynn, with a personal message, signed, and dated 1939.*

COST	● ● ●
OUTLOOK	● ●

ABOVE *The jewelry worn by Sophia Loren in the 1960 film* The Millionairess.

COST	● ●
OUTLOOK	● ●

ABOVE AND BELOW *Charlie Chaplin's hat, cane, and boots.*

COST	● ● ● ● ●
OUTLOOK	● ● ● ● ●

FAR RIGHT *Signed portrait study of a legendary beauty, Vivien Leigh.*

COST	● ● ●
OUTLOOK	● ●

RIGHT *Laurel and Hardy signed so many photographs that prices rarely rise high.*

COST	● ●
OUTLOOK	● ●

STAN LAUREL AND OLIVER HARDY

Mechanical Music & Records

POLYPHONES THAT PLAYED disks of popular music could be found in bars and saloons from the earliest years of the 20th century, and by 1910 the precursors of juke boxes — the first coin-in-the-slot music machines — were introduced.

At the same time street music was provided by barrel organs, some carried on the backs of the players, but others, like pianos, wheeled around on stands or drawn by ponies. The last of these only disappeared from the streets of some cities in the early 1960s. It is difficult to find any still in working condition, however, because hard wear and bad weather took their toll on the machinery.

The phonograph played cylinder records and enjoyed a fairly brief popularity, being displaced by the gramophone around 1914. The major manufacturer was Edison who produced the Standard, the Gem, the Home, the Fireside, and the Triumph. The ones that are most popular with collectors have large or elaborately shaped horns.

The gramophone had moved into homes by the time of World War I. "Gramophone" was a trade name registered by the Gramophone and Typewriter Company of the U.S. at the turn of the century but it quickly passed into everyday language to describe wind-up music players of flat records.

The most popular early gramophones are the ones that look most attractive, particularly the open-horn types. If there is painting on the horn, so much the better for the price. They were first produced by the Gramophone Company and later by His Master's Voice (HMV), which had the famous symbol of a listening dog as its trademark. The original picture of the dog, named Nipper, was painted by Francis Barraud in 1899.

Other gramophones included the Victor, produced in large numbers from 1905 onward, the Senior Monarch, and the Apollo, all popular with collectors, especially those in well-made, veneered cases. The Apollo was usually in a mahogany case.

Next to be developed were internal horn models, produced by HMV from the 1920s onward, and they can still be bought quite cheaply. HMV's No. 163 is very common but the 193/4 and the 202/3 are fairly rare. The re-entrant tone chamber cabinets, which HMV sold from 1928 to 1930, are favorites with collectors because of their fine tone.

Portable wind-up gramophones had a huge sale from the 1920s onward, and one of the most popular was the Aeolian Vocalion portable — those in hide cases sell for more than those in black cases. More recent record players, especially the Black Box record player of the late 1950s, in which records could be stacked to be played in turn, are currently rising in collecting status.

The growing popularity of the gramophone for in-home music meant that pianos began to disappear from most drawing rooms. In the 20th century pianos were usually made in traditional styles, with the exception of a few in chunky Art Deco style and some white-painted grand pianos that were popular with interior decorators between the wars. Later, very plain-cased pianos appeared.

Today, juke boxes from the 1950s and 1960s, especially the ones with flashing lights, are among the most coveted collectibles and fetch large sums of money.

The first vocal recordings were made in the U.S. in 1895 and in London in 1898, but for several years phonograph records were both rare and expensive. By 1904 the first singer to sell a million records was Caruso, and in 1910 the first double-sided disks were produced. From then the recording industry took off to become a multi-million earner.

The most obvious way to start any record collection is to concentrate on your own favorite groups and artists, but from there people go on to specialize in categories like folk, jazz, or disks made by particular groups. Some people collect records for their covers, and one of the most coveted is an original copy of *Sergeant Pepper's Lonely Hearts Club Band* with its collage

OPPOSITE *Brian Epstein's Presentation Gold Album for A Hard Day's Night by the Beatles, 1964.*

COST	● ● ● ● ●
OUTLOOK	● ● ● ●

LEFT *A table polyphon in a paneled walnut case.*

COST	● ● ●
OUTLOOK	● ● ● ●

BELOW *A Wurlitzer Model 780 — one of the most popular prewar jukeboxes.*

COST	● ● ● ●
OUTLOOK	● ● ●

cover by artist Peter Blake showing all the people that the Beatles most admired — including a plaster garden gnome.

Old single records were fragile and easily damaged, and frequently give poor, scratchy sound, so they are often not very expensive to buy. Artists like John McCormack, Richard Tauber, Flanagan and Allen, The Inkspots, and Gigli are among the most sought-after artists on old singles.

Early LPs were also made of thick celluloid and are liable to damage but they are treasured because they contain early jazz recordings by people like Louis Armstrong, Jack Teagarden, Bix Biederbecke, and Sidney Bechet. To be worth money they should still be in their original sleeves.

A record does not have to be old, however, to be worth collecting. Anything by Elvis Presley is now worth far more than was originally paid for it; so are almost all the recordings by the Beatles and Buddy Holly. Paul Anka and Abba, Talking Heads, and Lou Reed are all high in collecting favor. Cliff Richard's "Livin' Doll" brings a very high price, as does the LP "Love Child" by Diana Ross and the Supremes. Even records by artists who are still at the height of their fame like Michael Jackson are avidly collected and command high prices.

Movie Magazines & Music

FROM THEIR EARLY YEARS to the present day, movies have had magazines. In the beginning, and indeed up until the post-war period, these magazines tended to be of two types. There was the professional magazine for the distributor or movie house owner who needed to be informed as to what was coming onto the market, and through advertising persuaded to rent the films for showing. The other type is the more common, directed at the moviegoing public; these include magazines like *Picturegoer* with straightforward reviews and news of new films, and the American *Film Fun*, which is more concerned with photographs of leggy starlets. Persons with an interest in individual stars collect copies of magazines featuring them or the films they appeared in. Particularly collected are Marilyn Monroe and James Dean, and magazines featuring them rate about twice the normal price, while a magazine with just a Monroe cover will bring about $8. (Such is the magic of Monroe that the showgirl outfit she wore in the 1956 film *Bus Stop,* complete with its 20th Century Fox label, sold for around $25,000 at Sotheby's.)

Old piano stools are often treasure troves of yellowing sheaves of sheet music and some of them can be very valuable.

Music from the days of the music hall and the vaudeville show is, surprisingly, easier to find than sheet music from the 1950s onward. This is because, with the lower prices and accessibility of records, fewer people were actually making music themselves. After all, the 1950s and 1960s were the period when pianos could often only be sold for firewood.

Music with attractive covers commands the best prices. Geisha girl music sheets reflected the taste for all things Japanese at the beginning of the century; later covers echoed changes in fashion, and Jazz Age flappers can be seen kicking up their heels on music sheets of the Charleston. Music popularized by famous artists was also bought in large numbers — Marie Lloyd's pieces were good sellers as, slightly later, were the songs popularized by Al Jolson and Gracie Fields.

Early copies of sheet music for best-selling songs are often collected, particularly the work of Jerome Kern and Cole Porter, and so are songs made popular in films like *High Noon* and *Buttons and Bows.* Among the most expensive items of sheet music from recent times are Lonnie Donnegan's "Gamblin' Man," "Singing the Blues" as performed by Guy Mitchell and Tommy Steel, and anything by the Beatles.

Cards

VICTORIAN CHRISTMAS CARDS have been a favorite with collectors for some time, but there are also very pretty cards to be found dating from the 1920s and 1930s, when artists like Louis Wain and Mabel Lucie Attwell produced designs for manufacturers like Valentines of Dundee, one of the world's largest producers of greeting cards. In the inter-war period the verses inside cards became almost as important to buyers as the picture on the front, and manufacturers employed writers to turn out words that would sell their cards. Collectors should try to find the best of these because some of them were quite poetic.

Among the most sought-after cards of the 20th century are official" ones sent out by various organizations — clubs, hospitals, regiments, ships, colonial postings. A run of House of Commons cards, for example, would be sure to make money, as would a collection of the cards sent out by the various branches of the fighting forces and regiments in World War I. Cards signed by famous people are, as one would expect, highly collectible.

American tobacco and cigarette manufacturers, toward the end of the 19th century, were the first to hit on the idea of putting pictures on the pieces of card inserted to stiffen cigarette packets. Among the rarest and most valuable cards to be found today are the Sweet Caporal baseball cards issued around 1910 in honor of Honus Wagner, who played baseball from 1897 to 1917 and was held to be the greatest shortstop of all time.

The idea of using decorated cards as stiffeners for tobacco packets was taken up by a London tobacco, snuff, and tea merchant named James Taddy before the turn of the century. Taddy's brought out cards in sets of twenty and by 1920, when the company closed, it had produced numerous sets in categories like Clowns and Circus Artistes, Royalty, Actresses, Soldiers, Natives of the World, and Winners of the Victoria Cross.

W.D. & H.O. Wills also issued picture cards at an early date and continued to do so for many years. Their National Costumes in sets of twenty-five and their set of fifty Waterloo cards, brought out in 1915, are very valuable. The Waterloo set are hard to find because they were withdrawn from sale in deference to Britain's alliance with France during World War II.

Various companies produced over 5000 different sets of cards between them and collecting them became a very popular hobby, mostly with children but also with adults, until the end of World War I. Many of the cards were of a high artistic standard, and because most of them offered some information on the reverse side, they were a good source of

ABOVE *Card commemorating the visit of the Prince and Princess of Wales to India, 1905-6.*

COST	● ●
OUTLOOK	● ●

BELOW *Vacation humor on a postcard by Donald McGill.*

COST	● ●
OUTLOOK	● ●

I CAN'T SEE MY LITTLE JOHNNY !

PLAYER'S CIGARETTES

SCOTTISH MOUNTAIN, OR BLUE, HARE

ABOVE *A gift card issued in the 1920s and 30s by Player's cigarettes, depicting the Scottish mountain, or blue, hare.*

COST	● ●
OUTLOOK	● ●

OPPOSITE *Taddy cigarette cards — a full set of 20 Clowns and Circus Artistes, sold for a record price of around $26,000.*

COST	● ● ● ● ●
OUTLOOK	● ● ●

Valentines

The practice of sending Valentine cards is much older than that of sending Christmas cards. On February 14, young people have always eagerly awaited the visit of the mailman, and sometimes they were disappointed, especially if they received one of the "black" Valentines which were printed in large numbers during the 1920s and 1930s. These poked fun at the recipient, often in cruel terms, and, because the people who got them rarely kept them, they are hard to come across. Pretty, sentimental Valentines, however, were often treasured and those with embossed flowers, lace trimming, and sentimental verses are fairly easy to find. Some of the most popular were shaped like fans or cut-out flowers. For collectors, condition is very important.

general knowledge, covering a wide range of subjects from Wild Flowers to Air Raid Precautions and from How to Swim to Stars of Screen and Stage.

The condition of cards has a direct bearing on their value. Dog-eared, creased or marked sets are worth much less than those in pristine condition.

The first British postcard appeared in 1870 and was issued ready stamped by the General Post Office. It was not until the 1890s that independent companies began producing their own postcards for use with an adhesive stamp, and in 1902 an Act of Parliament was passed, allowing messages and addresses to be written on one side of a card, leaving the other side free for a picture.

Then the postcard as we know it today really took off and millions have been sold bearing every kind of picture imaginable. There are scenic postcards for places as far apart as Bombay and British Columbia; there are postcards with views of every village and hamlet in Britain; there are postcards of winsome ladies, movie stars, dogs, cheeky cartoons, ships, trains, automobiles, flowers; there are the sad little

postcards with printed messages to be ticked or crossed off, sent by soldiers at the Front during World War I.

Some collectors specialize in postcards of particular subjects, such as lighthouses or bridges, others in views of places where they spent their vacations as children. A favorite collecting subject is the French postcard of the 1920s which was famous for being "naughty." Although they are tame by today's standards, they showed naked or semi-naked ladies in provocative poses.

The postcards illustrated with comic cartoons were very popular, especially those by Donald McGill whose fat ladies and meek little husbands cavorted across millions of cards sent home from the beach by vacationers. Another popular illustrator of the 1930s was Lawson Wood, who drew comical cavemen building roadblocks or outwitting dinosaurs.

Some of the more expensive cards were embossed or embroidered and a few bore sprigs of real heather or Irish shamrocks. Some cards, such as C.W. Faulkner & Co.'s "Those Kids Again," were issued in sets of six, nine, or twelve and collectors endeavor to find them all.

Printed Ephemera

ABOVE *Ticket for the first commercial spaceflight, issued by Pan Am.*

COST	● ●
OUTLOOK	● ● ●

LEFT *Baggage labels and tickets from leisured days of prewar travel.*

COST	● ●
OUTLOOK	● ● ●

TAKE A CLOSE LOOK at the label on the next packet you buy in the supermarket. What does it say to you? Does it have visual appeal? It was dreamed up on a drawing board by an artist who wanted it to have enough impact for you to pick it off the shelf. There is a never-ending field of opportunities for label collecting and though most people tend to stick to labels from the past, there is no reason not to collect some of the effective labels that are being produced today.

Many of the most successful modern labels are versions of older ones. Mucha's Art Nouveau ladies, for example, are still used frequently. Camp Coffee's label has only been changed in minor details since the 19th century. Colman's mustard has labels based on ones from before the turn of the century. Often an old-fashioned look is a deliberate ploy to give the product "old time" status.

Some of the most attractive old labels are those from crates of fruit, especially oranges, though labels from apple crates and date boxes are also very interesting. In the early 20th century many orange growers bought their labels from printers in San Francisco who often sold the same picture to several different producers. Later, however, labels were made specifically for each grower.

Another source of attractive labels is cigar boxes which often bore richly embossed and very colorful labels, designed to give the effect of luxury. Modern cigar labels are still very attractive and repay interest.

The triangular stick-on labels that were put on portions of processed cheese were often charming. These can be found dating from the 1930s onward.

Tucked away in attics there may be suitcases plastered with luggage labels. Hotels and resorts all over the world used these as a form of advertising before and immediately after World War II. Some of these labels were extremely well designed and make a very interesting subject for collecting.

Packaging from the past is also worthy of interest. Black Cat cigarettes, popular in the 1930s, had a simple, eye-catching packet in red with a silhouette of a cat on it. Passing Cloud cigarettes had a very stylish packet that must have contributed greatly to their appeal.

Ephemera are the bits and pieces of paper that usually end up thrown into wastebaskets, but occasionally some are kept and in time pay their own mute tribute to the past.

Who saved a weighing machine ticket from the Titanic? Someone did. Who saved a ticket from the last trolley to run in Edinburgh? Who saved a ticket from the first electrified train to run in Britain? An awareness of the possible significance of certain bits of paper has given us some of the more unusual pieces of printed ephemera. Or sometimes printed ephemera are saved by accident, stuck in the backs of drawers, stored in attics, used as a lining for trunks or boxes.

Ration books from World War II are valuable collectibles today — although everyone had a ration book, only a few were

TOP LEFT *World War II ration books — the kind of ephemera to collect for posterity.*

COST	●●
OUTLOOK	●●●●

ABOVE *Travel labels and badges.*

COST	●●
OUTLOOK	●●●

LEFT *American War Bonds Certificate — attractive to collect.*

COST	●●
OUTLOOK	●●●●

kept after the war ended. It is possible to collect ephemera throughout your life — gas coupons printed for people in certain jobs during the oil crisis of the 1970s but never actually used are among present-day collectibles.

The range of possible ephemera is enormous and includes football match posters, notices for auction sales, old newspapers, theater bills and publicity handouts, trade catalogs, accounts, and menu cards. The person who kept some of the menu cards Charles Rennie Mackintosh's wife Margaret Macdonald designed for Miss Cranston's tearooms in Glasgow saved very valuable bits of paper indeed.

When saving ephemera, it is necessary to specialize or the collection will engulf your living space. Start keeping bits of paper with interesting information and attractive graphics or pieces that relate to some significant historical event, and future collectors will have reason to thank you.

Busted bonds are scraps of paper that represent lost fortunes and doomed hopes. The early 20th century was a boom time for floating new companies and persuading the public to put money into money-making enterprises, not all of which lived up to expectations. It was not that all the investments that people made were of doubtful legality, for some of the most sought-after "busted bonds" were issued by governments but were swept away by the tide of history.

For example, 1912 City of Nickoleaf bonds were sold extensively, as were bonds for the 1910 launch of the Troitzk

Railway and the Kokard to Namangan Railway, but within a few years the Russian Revolution swept away all hope of bond-holders earning a cent from their investments. Recently collectors started paying good prices for attractive bond and share certificates, and though the Russian government has announced that it is prepared to pay some reparation to certain pre-Revolution bond-holders, it is sometimes more profitable to sell them as collectors' items.

The Chinese Imperial Government was another popular market for investment that did not pay out on its potential, and bonds for the Anglo-German Gold Loan issued by the Deutsche-Asiatische Bank are worth collecting for their appearance alone.

Other share certificates and bonds that proved to be bad investments at the time but are now worth money were those issued in the 1920s by golf clubs, greyhound tracks, and racecourses that did not survive the Great Depression.

Old share certificates are often very attractively engraved but they must be in good condition to be worth collecting.

Posters

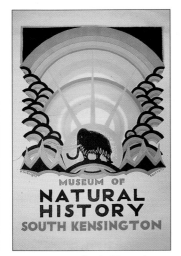

ABOVE *Poster for the Natural History Museum in London by McKnight Kauffer.*

COST	● ●
OUTLOOK	● ● ●

TOULOUSE-LAUTREC was more famous in his own time for his *Folies Bergère* posters than he was for his paintings, and Alphonse Mucha's tendril-haired women advertising soap or perfumes are still fervently admired and collected. But perhaps the most successful mini-poster ever dreamed up was Milton Glaser's deceptively simple "I ♥ NY". It has been copied all over the world for every possible thing that anybody could love.

The power of the poster is infinite, whether it is in the business of selling political propaganda or advertising soap. Posters have undergone many changes of style and fashion, but, since their aim is impact, the most successful ones have been those that appealed, with directness and simplicity, to mass audiences. World War I poster with Lord Kitchener pointing an accusing finger at every passer-by raised recruiting figures with its powerful blackmail. The posters commissioned by the Shell Gas company helped to make it a commercial success. They used artists like Rex Whistler, Nicolas Bentley, and Edward Bawden in the 1930s, and in the 1960s Esso had a runaway success with its "Put a Tiger In Your Tank" poster.

ABOVE *Cunard poster for a New World cruise.*

COST	● ●
OUTLOOK	● ● ●

LEFT *Rijksmuseum, Amsterdam poster, Studio Dumbar, Holland, 1986.*

COST	● ●
OUTLOOK	● ● ●

OPPOSITE *Festival of Britain poster, 1951.*

COST	● ●
OUTLOOK	● ● ●

LEFT *Advertisement for the Chicago World's Fair that celebrated a century of progress: 1833-1933.*

COST	● ●
OUTLOOK	● ● ●

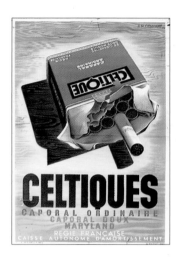

Another patron of the telling poster was London Transport which employed Edward Bawden, John Minton, and Edward McKnight Kauffer to put its message across to the public. Perhaps the most successful poster it produced was the logical and easy-to-understand Underground map, drawn in 1933 by H.C. Beck and still used in its original form.

Poster collectors have a vast field from which to choose — for example, World War II posters saying "Join the Wrens," "Beat Firebomb Fritz," or Fougasse's "Careless Talk Costs Lives"; American posters designed by Norman Rockwell or James Montgomery, who dreamed up the "Uncle Sam" figure; Dick Wilkinson's posters of strength-filled workmen for Guinness, and the magnificent posters done for the ocean liner, the *Normandie,* by French artist A.M. Cassandre, who will ever be remembered as the man who produced the "Dubo — Dubon — Dubonnet" poster.

Comics & Magazines

ABOVE British TV Comic *No. 1, featuring Muffin the Mule.*

COST	● ●
OUTLOOK	● ● ● ●

1938 WAS THE red-letter year of the comic world because it saw the birth of the famous American *Action* comics in which Superman made his debut. In the same year D.C. Thomson of Dundee launched its *Dandy* and *Beano* for the children of Britain.

The idea of publications aimed at children was not new, because English journalist Arthur Mee had launched *The Children's Newspaper* in 1908. It was a serious, educative publication, much approved of by parents, who tended to look down their noses at the cheerful, colorful nonsense of the comics that, of course, children much preferred. In the 1910s and 20s several comics had appeared, including *Funny Cuts, Comic Cuts, Chips*, and *Ally Sloper*, but they did not achieve the popularity of their successors.

American comics were the most popular of all. Superman, created by Joe Schuster and Jerry Seigal, started a trend that was followed up in comics like *Black Cobra, Yellow Jacket, Black Hood, Dick Tracey*, and *Batman*. Movie star heroes like Roy Rogers had comics dedicated to them and their adventures, while numerous comics issued by the Walt Disney corporation featured its cartoon characters.

OPPOSITE BELOW *Wartime humour: "No Gum Chum" cartoons, 1945.*

COST	● ●
OUTLOOK	● ● ● ●

BELOW LEFT Superman, Batman, Wonder Woman *action comics.*

COST	●
OUTLOOK	● ● ● ●

BELOW Eagle, *featuring Dan Dare, Beano, and* Dandy *— these are the British children's comic classics.*

COST	● ●
OUTLOOK	● ● ● ●

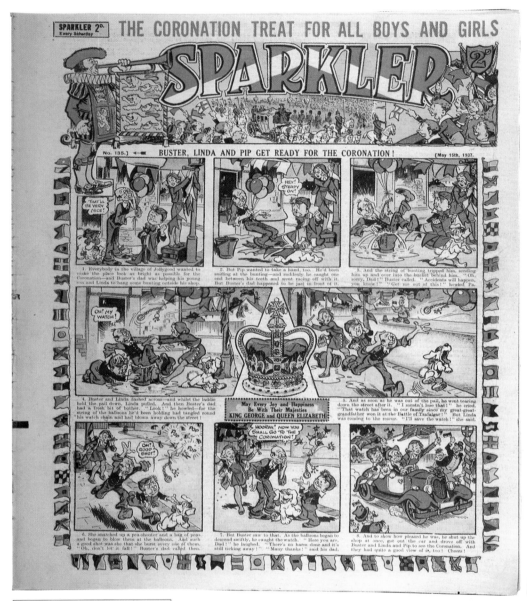

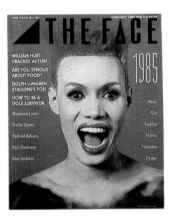

People tend to buy magazines that inform them about subjects of particular interest. Anyone who had the foresight to stash away early auto magazines will today have a valuable archive; so will the buyer of early issues of news or satirical magazines, such as Britain's *Private Eye*. That magazine's own personal ads always carry ads asking for specific back numbers to add to some enthusiast's collection.

When building up a magazine collection it is best to aim for a run over several years — from the very beginning is ideal. However, magazines from specific phases of the publication's existence can be valuable. Copies of *Vogue* or *Harper's Bazaar* from the early 1920s and 1930s are collector's items today because of their eye-catching covers, many of which were designed by famous artists. Another magazine treasured for its covers is *The Ladies' Home Journal*, for which Norman Rockwell did many magnificent paintings.

First Editions

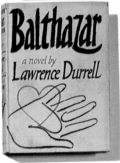

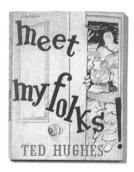

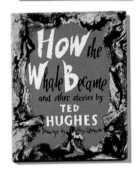

"CONDITION" IS THE KEY WORD as far as collecting modern first editions is concerned. For a book to be worth money it should have its original dust jacket and the neater and less tattered that is, the better. In fact a dust jacket in good condition is generally worth half the purchase price of the book and on occasion is worth far more. For example, a first edition copy of Aldous Huxley's *Brave New World* will sell for around $16 without its dust jacket but for $160 with it.

In order for a first edition to make a good price, the binding must look as pristine as possible, the spine must be unbroken and the book should still have its endpapers. A valuable first edition should be preserved in as close to its original published state as possible. It is also preferable if some previous owner has not signed the flyleaf or allowed the children to draw in the margins. If the previous owner is someone famous, however, a bookplate or a signature will add to the value of the book and if it is an author-signed copy, preferably with a fond dedication to another famous person, the price goes up even more.

As far as first edition collectors are concerned, the prestige of an author rises and falls in an unpredictable way. One year Arnold Bennett is sought after, the next year he is out. The appearance of an acclaimed biography, a centenary or a literary scandal can put up the price of first editions and some writers like T.S. Eliot or J.P. Sartre hold their place against allcomers. Generally speaking, however, the more prolific and popular the author in his or her lifetime, the lower the price of first editions because published works were likely to have been produced in large print runs. Sometimes the little-regarded first book of an author who later achieved acclaim can be very collectible.

Authors do not have to be dead and buried for their books to be valuable and collectors with an eye to profit should look out for Lawrence Durrell, particularly the first editions of his *Alexandria Quartet*, and the early works of Christopher Isherwood whose seventy-cent edition of *Sally Bowles*, published in 1937, is today worth upward of $250.

Anyone setting out to invest in books might go for hardcover literary prizewinners. For example, Salman Rushdie's 1981 winner of the Booker Prize, *Midnight's Children*, increased in price ten times over six years.

ABOVE *First editions of Lawrence Durrell's* Alexandria Quartet.

| COST | ● ● |
| OUTLOOK | ● ● |

ABOVE *First editions of children's books by poet Ted Hughes.*

| COST | ● ● |
| OUTLOOK | ● ● |

BELOW *First edition of* The Waves *by Virginia Woolf, produced by the Hogarth Press.*

COST	● ● ●
OUTLOOK	● ● ●

RIGHT *First edition of* 1984 *by George Orwell.*

COST	● ● ●
OUTLOOK	● ● ●

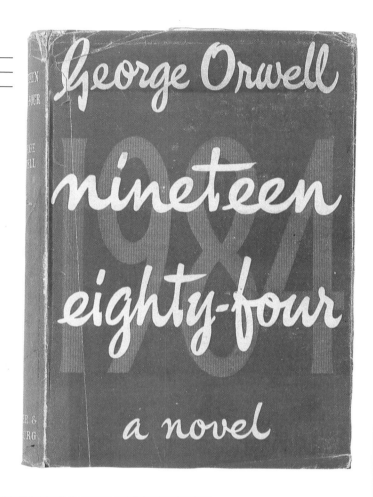

Autograph letters

Original letters and documents written or signed by the famous names of history — great authors, naval and military leaders, kings and queens, scientists, artists, and musicians — provide a fascinating field for the private collector as well as the raw material for historical research.

The value of any letter or document will depend on many factors, most importantly the identity of the writer and the scarcity of the signature. In addition, the contents and condition are significant and must always be taken into account.

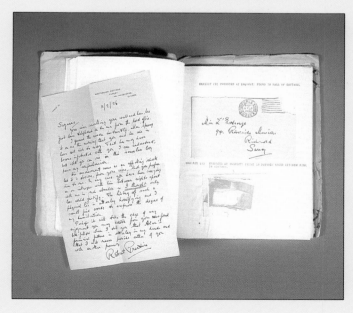

There is a particular demand for literary letters and for royal documents, but any piece of paper or parchment bearing a famous name is likely to be of some value. A signed letter from Winston Churchill could easily command about $850, but occasionally a real gem comes onto the market, such as the letter from Albert Einstein, dated August 2, 1939, to President Roosevelt concerning the discovery of nuclear fission and advising the urgent development of the atomic bomb. That sold at Christie's for some $250,000.

Index

Acknowledgments

Quarto would like to thank the following for their help with this publication and for permissions to reproduce copyright material.
Abbreviations used:
a = above, *b* = below, *c* = center, *l* = left, *r* = right

Aldus = Aldus Archives
Bridgeman = Bridgeman Art Library
Christies = Christies Colour Library
Corning = Corning Museum of Glass
DC = Design Council
Duncan = Alastair Duncan
Hornak = Angelo Hornak
J&L = John Jesse and Irina Laski
Opie = Robert Opie
V and A = Victoria and Albert Museum

p1: J & L; p2: J & L; p4: DC; p5: Christies; p6: 20th Century Box; p7: DC; p8: Christies; p10: *al* Christies, *c* Nicholas Pine, *b* Christies; p11: *row 1 l* Hornak, *r* DC, *row 2 l* Christies, *r* Lewis Kaplan, London, *row 3 l* Royal Doulton, *r* DC, *row 4 l* DC, *c* Max Protech, New York, *r* Garth Clark Gallery, New York; p12: *l* Duncan, *r* Hornak; p13: *l* Hornak, *r* Royal Doulton, *b* Royal Worcester Spode, pp14-15: Royal Doulton; p16: Christies; p17: *al* Aldus, *ar* Duncan, *b* Christies; p18: Christies; p19: *bl* Hornak, *a* DC, *br* Christies; p20: *l and c* Royal Doulton, *r* DC; p21: *a* DC, *cl* Wedgwood, *cr* 20th Century Box, *b* Opie; p22: Nicholas Pine; p23: *a* Nicholas Pine, *b* Deirdre O'Day; p24: Barbara Berg, Chenil Galleries; p25: *al* 20th Century Box, *ar* Christies, *b* Garth Clark Gallery, New York; p26: *l* Jane Peiser, *r* Janice Tchalenko; p27: *bl* Christies, *c* DC; p28: Corning; p30: *row 1* Corning, *row 2* Galerie Moderne, London, *rows 3 and 4* Corning; p31: *row 1 l* Christies, *r* Hornak, *row 2 l* Corning, *c* Corning, *r* Christies, *row 3 l* Corning, *c* Lewis Kaplan, *row 4 c* Corning, *r* Corning, p32: Christies; p33: *cl* Christies, *ar* Galerie Moderne, London, *bl* Galerie Moderne, London, *br* Hornak; p34: Christies; p35: *l* Christies, *ac* Christies, *ar* Corning, *b* Aldus; p36: Corning; p37: *al* Corning/Rockwell Museum, *ar* Corning/gift Mrs C L Dencenburg, *bl* Donald Hall/Rochester, New York, *br* Duncan; p38: *l* Corning, *c* Lewis Kaplan, London, *r* Christies; p39: *a* Christies, *b* Aldus, p40: *l* Corning, *r* Corning, p41: *al* Corning, *bl* Corning/Rockwell Museum, *cr* Hornak, *br* Opie; p42 *b* Christies, *ar* Corning, *b* Christies; p43: *l and r* Corning, p44: Cassina; p46: *a* DC, *b* Duncan, p47: *row 1 l* Christies, *r* Aldus, *row 2 l* DC, *c* Hornak, *r* Musée des Arts Decoratifs, Paris, *row 3 l* David Linley Company, *c and r* Hornak; p48: DC; p49: *al* Aldus, *b* Deidi von Schaewen, p50: *b* Christies; p51: *a* Christies, *bl* Christies, *br* Hornak, p52: *l* David Linley Company, *r* Duncan, p53: *l* Hornak, *r* Aldus, p54: *al* Christies, *ar* Hornak, *bl* Aldus, *br* Fisher Fine Art, London, p55: Duncan; p56: *l* Aldus, *c* DC, *r* Christies, p57: *a* Aldus, *bl* Aldus, *br* Cassina; p58: Christies; p59: *l* Aldus; *r* Christies, p60: Bridgeman; p62: *a* Christies, *c* The Patchwork Dog and Calico Cat, *bc* Aldus, p63: *row 1 l* Christies, *c* Hornak, *r* Musée des Arts Decoratifs, Paris, *row 2 l* DC, *row 3 l* Liberty, *c* Corning, *r* Laura Ashley/Andreas von Einsieder, p64: *c* Hornak, *bl* Christies, *br* Aldus; p65: *al* Musée des Arts Decoratifs, Paris, *b* Christies, p66: *l* E T Archive, *r* The Patchwork Dog and Calico Cat; p67: *a and b* E T Archive, *ar* Christies, p68: *a* Christies, *b* Hornak, *ar* Hornak, *b* Bridgeman; p69: *al* Hornak, *ar* Hornak, *b* Bridgeman; p70: *l* Hornak, *c* Christies; p71: *a* Christies, *b* Aldus, p72: Hornak; p74: *a* Hornak, *c* Aldus, *b* DC; p75: DC; p76: DC; p77: Aldus; p78: Aldus; p79 *a* Aldus, *cl* Opie; p80: *a* Jesse & Laski, *b* Aldus; p81: DC;

p83: *al* DC, *cl* DC, *bl* E T Archive, *ac* DC, *bc* DC, *r* DC; p84: *l* Christies, *b* Bridgeman; p85: *al* Christies, *ar* Hornak, *cr* DC, *b* Aldus, p86: *a* Toy Museum, *b* Sothebys; p87: *l* Christies, *ar* Phillips, *b* Toy Museum, p88: Hornak; p90: *a* Christies, *b* Aldus, p91: *row 1 l* Christies, *r* Christies, *row 2 l* Hornak, *c* Duncan, DC, *row 3 c* Aldus, *r* DC, *row 4 r* Aldus, p92: *l* Hornak, *r* Hornak, p93: Christies; p94: Aldus; p95 *l* E T Archive, *r* Christies, p96: Christies; p97: *al* Aldus, *bl* Hornak; p98: *l* Bridgeman, *r* E T Archive, p99 *l and a* Hornak, *c* David Gill, *bc* Barbara Berg, Chenil Galleries, London, *br* Hornak; p100: Christies; p102: *a* Wartskis, London, *c* Sothebys, *b* J & L; p103: *row 1 l* The Purple Shop, *c* Christies, *row 2 l* J & L, *c* La Verité Ltd, London, *r* J & L, *row 3* J & L, *row 4* Lesley Craze Gallery, London, p104: *al* Beaux Bijoux, London, p105: *bl* Sarah Dwyer & Tony Giorgi, London, *r* J & L, *l* DC, *al* L'Odeon, London, *ar* Hornak; p106: *b* J & L, p107: *al* J & L, *ar* Musée des Arts Decoratifs, Paris, p107: *c* Christies, *bl* J & L, *br* The Purple Shop, p108: *al* La Verité Ltd, *c* Geoff Roberts, *b* J & L, p109: *l* V and A, *ar* Deirdre O'Jay, *c* Sarah Dwyer & Tony Giorgio, London, *b* Worshipful Company of Goldsmiths; p110: *l* J & L, *r* Christies; p111: *a* Christies, *b* The Purple Shop, London; p112: *l* J & L, *ar* J & L, *br* Lesley Craze Gallery, London, p113: *l* Beaux Bijoux, London, *r* J & L; p114: E T Archive, p116: Sothebys; p117: *row 1 l* E T Archive, *r* Hornak, *row 2 l* 20th Century Box, London, *c* Persiflage, London, *row 3 l* Stanhope Bowry, London, *r* P O'Day, *row 4 l* Zandra Rhodes, *c* J & L, *r* 20th Century Box, London; p118: *l* E T Archive, *c* Aldus, *r* Christies; p119: Aldus; p120: *l* Sothebys, *r* Keystone Collection; p121: *l* Keystone Collection, *r* Aldus, *br* 20th Century Box, London, p122: *l* Sothebys, *r* E T Archive, p123: *l* E T Archive, *r* Sothebys, p124: *r* Sothebys; p125: *l* Sothebys, *ar* Sothebys, *br* Keystone Collection; p126 *l* Persiflage, London, *ar* Sothebys, *bl* The Patchwork Dog and Calico Cat, London, p127: *l* E T Archive, *r* Keystone Collection, p128: *l* 20th Century Box, *r* Stanhope Bowry, London; p129: *bl* Christies, *c* Barbara Berg, Chenil Galleries, *r* La Verité Ltd, London; p130: *l* Hornak, *ar* Persiflage, *b* Persiflage, London, p131: Persiflage; p132: Sothebys; p134: *row 1* Sothebys, *row 2* Toy Museum, *row 3* Geoff & Linda Price, *row 4* DC; p135: *row 1 l* Christies, *r* Toy Museum, *row 2 l* Toy Museum, *row 3* Christies, *r* DC, *row 4 l* Toy Museum, p137: *a* Sothebys, *cl* DC, *cr* Toy Museum, *b* DC; p138: *a* Sothebys, *b* V and A; p140: *a* Toy Museum, *b* Toy Museum, p141: Toy Museum, p142: *al* Christies, *bl* Sothebys, *c* Toby Haggith, *r* Christies; p143: Christies; p144 *a* Phillips, *b* Sothebys, p145: *al* 20th Century Box, London, *cl* 20th Century Box, London, *bl* DC, *ar* Toy Museum, *br* Opie; p146: *a* Christies, *bl* Sothebys, *br* Christies; p147: *l* Phillips, *ar* Christies, *cr* Christies, *br* Toby Haggith, p148: *l* Sothebys, *r* DC, *a* Hornak, *b* DC, p150: Phillips, p152: *a* E T Archive, *c* Author's collection, *b* Noel Tovey; p153: *row 1 l* Jean-Loup Charmet, *c* E T Archive, *r* Aldus, *row 2 l* Jean-Loup Charmet, *r* E T Archive, *row 3 l* Aldus, *row 3 r* Opie, *row 4 l* Sothebys; p154: *a* Phillips, *b and l* Sothebys; p155: Sothebys; p156: *a* Christies, *b* Sothebys; p157: Christies; p158: *a* Sothebys, *l* Christies, *b* Trevor Martin; p160 *l and c* Aldus, *r* Opie; p161: Aldus; p162: *a and b* E T Archive, *ar* Aldus; p163: *l* Phillips, *r* Opie; p164: *l* Aldus, *r* Opie; p165: *a and b* Aldus, *r* Opie; p166: *al* Opie, *bl* Western Americana, *ar* Opie; p167: *l* Aldus, *ar* E T Archive, *br* Jean-Loup Charmet; p168: *a* Aldus, *b and r* Author's collection, p169: Aldus; p170: Aldus; p171: *l* Aldus, *r* Author's Collection; Jacket: *row 1, airplane*, W. Anderson, *r* Christies, *cover* Angelo Hornak, *r bracelets*, J & L, *row 4, silver dish*, Lewis Kaplan Associates, *row 5, c, jewelry on sculpture*, Angelo Hornak, *r, chair*, Knoll International, *back of jacket*, Trevor Martin.

Every effort has been made to trace and acknowledge all copyright holders. Quarto would like to apologize if any omissions have been made.